The Wor

Yoga for the Brain™

Cristina Smith

Rick Smith

Darity Wesley

Published by Cristina Smith
Nevada City, CA 95959
www.SudokuWisdom.com

Published by Sudoku Wisdom

ISBN: 978-1544211558

Stay Sharp! Have Fun! Pencil Me In!

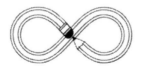

Table of Contents

Introduction

Ever meet someone for the first time and feel like you have known them forever? Felt that the profound heart and soul connection somehow transcends time and space? I had that extraordinary experience when I met our guest artist Darity Wesley 20 some years ago.

Over our years of friendship, we have worked together, appeared on stages around the country together and supported causes together. We even served as consecutive presidents of our local League of Women Voters. Our collaboration on The Word Search Oracle is yet another beautiful blossoming of our treasured alliance.

A Modern Day Oracle™, Darity shares her unique talent of blending business and spiritual pursuits. Legal counsel to a wide spectrum of global clients, she incorporates her wisdom teachings into all circumstances. Darity is a dynamic speaker at conferences nationwide, on a number of topics including death. (We call her the Death Diva!) She writes and offers her Oracle messages to the benefit of her global community. Darity is an avid supporter and facilitator of the new reality.

Darity's Oracle guidance gives us a compass to help navigate the waters of our ever-evolving world. These messages shine as a north star of ongoing support to assist us in cultivating a connection with our own eternal essence.

In this collaboration, Darity offers us mini-Oracles, condensed versions of her original in-depth readings. Our Puzzle Master Rick has taken these minis and created fabulously fun word search puzzles. To top it all off, at the end of each puzzle there is a powerful secret message to decode.

What is an Oracle?

Many of us have had Oracle experiences, though we may not have called them that. Have you had the feeling there's a guardian angel looking out for you? Or heard an inner voice that is not your own? Gotten a profound insight that you would not have otherwise considered? Had your prayers answered? Especially in an unexpected way? These are a few of the ways that the invisible world guides us.

Children frequently communicate directly with these allies that grown-ups call imaginary friends, often giving them a name. Maybe you did too, when you were young?

A few people kept their direct contact with the unseen world as they matured, or have reconnected with it as adults. They are the modern day oracles. Their gift is to decipher messages from angels, guides and allies, to help us translate these blessings into our daily lives.

For thousands of years, most cultures have included Oracles as respected members of the community. Look at Moses with the divine revelation of the Ten Commandments.

The Greek Oracle at Delphi, known as the Pythia, were consulted by commanders, kings and commoners. From the Sybils of early Rome to ancient Chinese bone readers to Nostradamus to the Celtic Druids, Oracles have influenced and advised people, created events, made decisions and changed history itself. More recently Edgar Cayce and others have shared their wisdom and molded our world. Even the Dalai Lama has his own oracle, the Nechung Oracle of Tibet.

These translators of the divine enter a meditative state where they are able to bypass brain chatter. They listen beyond ears, and see with eyes closed. Many of our greatest philosophies and inventions have been brought forth from the unseen via an Oracle messenger.

Can we, as individuals, begin to train ourselves to explore that objective listening state of awareness beyond daily life? Yes! Darity would counsel that we have only to listen to the still, quiet voice within...

Play with this book and discover the truth for yourself.

Your own internal Oracle might surprise you.

How to Use This Oracle

Dive right in! Soak in the Oracle readings. Have fun solving all of these deliciously unique puzzles and inspiring secret messages. Decode the hidden mantra and feel like you are doing a magic card trick or making the letters written in invisible ink mysteriously appear.

Choose you own pace. You are welcome to zip right through this book or take your time. Each Word Search Oracle is designed to be a spiritual mindfulness practice that will enhance your life. These meditations can open the door to higher awareness and provoke profound inner exploration. Relax. Savor the process. There is no need to rush.

Each Oracle creates specific benefits. First reading initiates the overall focus of the meditation. The carefully selected word list supports different facets of the theme. Solving the puzzle itself improves whole brain health function and flexibility. Finally, the deciphered mantra reveals a powerful affirmation that can embed these positive messages into the essence of everyday life.

These modern day Oracle mantras are a blend of traditional mantras and affirmations. They are designed to be repeated over and over again, both silently and aloud. Recite out loud when you are in the car. Say them soundlessly in your head while doing mundane tasks like washing the dishes and cleaning.

Mantras can help keep your mind doing something wonderful and beneficial rather than driving you nuts. Take that, monkey mind!

Choose a Word Search Oracle for the day or week or to help deal with a particular situation. Read it more than once. Let the full meaning sink in. Do the mantra for a while. Watch what happens. Play and work with it over time. Let the layers of understanding guide your next step. Follow your intuition!

Many roads lead to the key.

Be flexible on the path.

Let's Play!

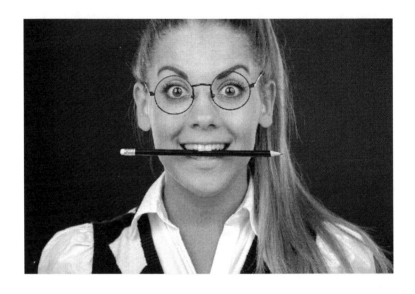

Mark up your book!

Play with the Oracles!

Make Mistakes!

Have Fun!

How to Play

A word search puzzle consists of letters placed in a grid. Some of the letters form words, others not. The object of this game is to find and mark all the words hidden inside the grid that appear in the accompanying word list. The words may be placed horizontally, vertically, or diagonally, and arranged forward or backward, depending on the difficulty level of the puzzle.

There are three levels of puzzles. The first 10 puzzles will get you started. The words you are looking for in the grid are spelled forward. They are either in a horizontal or vertical line and no letters are shared by other words.

The next 10 puzzles, 11-20, add a new level of challenge. There are a few more words hidden in the grid. They are not only horizontal or vertical; they could also be found diagonally. Some words may share letters. All of the words are spelled forward.

Puzzles 21-60 are the most advanced. There are even more words hidden in the grid and they might be backward as well as forward.

Hidden within the puzzle is a secret message created by the letters that are not used in any word within the grid. The key to decoding it is underneath the text of the reading. The blank lines are where you will place the letters discovered once the word search phase of the puzzle is complete.

Starting from the top left corner of the puzzle grid and proceeding left to right, line by line, place each unused letter in the blank in order. When solved, a mantra associated with the Oracle reading magically appears!

Let the mystery reveal itself.

It can surprise you.

How to Find the Words

Knowing where to start is sometimes
the key to the solution.

There is no one right way to solve these word search puzzles. It's individual. Your unique brilliance will reveal your perfect way forward. Word search puzzles are a wonderful way to play with your brain and help increase its flexibility. Experiment with these different strategies and notice how it feels when doing each. It is likely that one approach will feel more natural.

What's great about playing with your brain in this context is that it is a no-risk proposition. Nothing critical is on the line. There is no deadline. No one else will be judging your performance. It is the perfect laboratory in which to do research on yourself. A whole brain approach could look something like this:

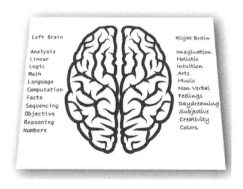

Start with the right brain intuitive approach. Read the Oracle message. Scan the grid and see what words you notice first. Circle them, then cross them off the list. It is interesting to make a note of the ones that pop out at as an indicator of your current state of being.

Take a look at the word list and then look again at the grid and see what else reveals itself. Consider picking out a word and see if you are able to find it by shifting your perspective.

Next, move to the left brain logical strategy. A common tactic for finding all the words is to go through the puzzle left to right (or vice versa) and look for the first letter of the word. After finding the letter, look at the eight surrounding letters to see whether the next letter of the word is there. Continue this system until the entire word is found.

The step by step method approaches the word list in order. It's helpful to skip over the ones that are elusive at the moment and come back to those words later.

Which words did you have a hard time finding? Notice anything interesting about them? Isn't it fascinating what we see and don't see?

Get to know yourself in different states of mind.

New perspectives emerge.

Colorful Tip

Many people use a pencil to circle found words and then cross or check them off the list. That works well, especially if you have a good eraser. However, the grid looks a bit chaotic when all of the word list is found. As a colorful tip, use a highlighter felt tip pen to identify found words in the grid. It can make it easier to recognize which letters remain unused when decoding the secret message.

Set yourself up for success in all aspects of your life.

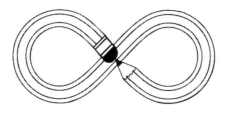

Blessings

The blessings in our lives sustain us, even when we or someone close to us is in pain or having difficult times. Move deeper inside. Rediscover spirit. Awaken more and more to living in a meaningful relationship with Source. There are many blessings every day. Open to this inner core.

Take a look around. There are so many things to be grateful for. Appreciate the good things, the love and joy. Having a thankful heart lifts our spirit and supports our journey.

Mantra:

— ——————— —— ————

—————————— ————

—————————

```
L I F E R A W A K E N J I
E M B R E R A O D H C O E
M Y I M L E A P E E T U M
N Y N B A D B E E A H R E
S L N E T I L N P R A N A
U S E B I S E S U R S K N
S T P I I N O S P N G F I
A I L N S V I P W I U T N
I R I G H E N O H G L R G
N I F A I R G R C O R E U
T T T I P T S T G O O D L
U D A P P R E C I A T E E
```

Appreciate   Heart   Rediscover
Awaken   Inner   Relationship
Blessings   Journey   Spirit
Bring   Life   Support
Core   Lift   Sustain
Deeper   Meaningful   Thankful
Good   Open

Relaxation

Take time to reacquaint yourself with your inner nature through relaxation.

Let go of everything, including the pain, sorrow, or disconnectedness. Take some deep breaths. Feel. Spend time in nature. Allow nature to fill your soul. All is happening just as it is supposed to, even though we may not know why. Release it all and breathe. Relax into being who you are.

Mantra:

— —— ——————— ———— —————— —— ——— —————— —————

```
I A D B E I N G K N O W M
R E I P A I N I N N E R E
L V S R R E L A X A X F I
N E C E G T B F E E L I H
I R O A N A R D E E P L A
T Y N C O K E M T Y S L P
S T N Q E E A L I F O S P
I H E U N T T H M E R O E
P I C A R E H S E E R U N
N N T I T M E W H Y O L I
O G E N N A T U R E W M N
E N D T S U P P O S E D G
R E L E A S E A L L O W T
```

Allow	Happening	Sorrow
Being	Inner	Soul
Breathe	Know	Supposed
Deep	Nature	Take
Disconnected	Pain	Time
Everything	Reacquaint	Why
Feel	Relax	
Fill	Release	

3   The Power of Presence

Be present. Keep attention focused on what is, as opposed to what could be or should be or would be.

The power of being present is transformative. The mind likes to take us on merry rides, either forward or back in time. Neither are here now. To be present, begin by bringing awareness and attention fully into where you are and who you are with. Focus the mind on the here and now. Ignore any distractions.

When we pay attention, through our thoughts and feelings, to what is happening in this moment, we are present. Present to listen to others. Present to listen to ourselves. Present to listen to the small voice within, spirit, intuition, which guides and directs choices. Presence brings the power to make choices based on the now. The concentrated force of our full attention on what truly is transcends limitation. Are you ready to work with the power that comes with that focus?

Mantra:

—   ——————   ——   —————   ——
———   —————   ——
————————   ——   ———   ———
——   ————   ——

```
I C P H O M O M E N T O F
S E O T O D W I T H I N O
W E W L L F O R W A R D C
I N E T A B H C O U L D U
T G R E T A F O R C E S S
H U T A C T E R I D E O
O I F P E K T I M E R E S
U D S E N S H O U L D N C
G E M E T T O M E R R Y S
H V A A I S P I R I T Y Y
T O L E O S T W O U L D O
S I L W N P R E S E N C E
H C I N T U I T I O N A T
I E S L I S T E N F E E L
```

Attention	Intuition	Small
Back	Listen	Spirit
Could	Merry	Thoughts
Feel	Moment	Time
Focus	Power	Voice
Force	Presence	Within
Forward	Ride	Would
Guide	Should	

Support

Sometimes we all think that we are just going along, hoping, praying, trusting and believing that we are on the right path. Trust yourself. You are wonderful! Your life's mission is important! You are totally supported by your angels, guides, and loved ones on the other side. Many entities and levels of consciousness are all cheering you on. Step by step.

You are truly unconditionally supported much more than you can even imagine. You are supported in taking steps to move yourself into newer, truer directions. Your growth will be exponential! You are becoming more and more your authentic self. Keep focused. Stay in the here and now. Know that you are completely and truly loved.

Mantra:

— —— ————————————————— —
————— —— —— ———————
—————— ———— ——— ———
— —— ————————— ——
————

```
I A F O C U S E D M O R E M
M I S S I O N U N C I O N D
I T E N T I T I E S M I O N
S U P P O R T A T L A L Y L
O H O P E V A W R E G D B Y
U N P M Y U U O U N I S E E
N E R N S U T N E P N P O R
S W A T T E H D R A E M A N
E E Y R D F E E A N G E L S
E R I I L O N R G U I D E S
N W N G M Y T F G R O W T H
G R G H A T I U P A T H I T
U D E T T O C L S E L F T H
C H E E R I N G S T E P E M
```

Angels	Hope	Right
Authentic	Imagine	Self
Cheering	Mission	Step
Entities	More	Support
Focused	Newer	Truer
Growth	Path	Unseen
Guides	Praying	Wonderful

5   Fearlessness

We've come a long way since scientists were convinced that the only reaction our little lizard brain has to fearful situations is either fight or flight. Now we are exploring psychologically, psychically and spiritually the aspects, experiences and manifestations of fear and our ability to transmute it into fearlessness!

Part of the practice of fearlessness is confronting the voice inside our heads that keeps telling us, "You might make a mistake! Boy, will you be sorry!" You know the one I'm talking about, the one who tells you, "What's going to happen if…?"

Stand up to it. Tell that voice "Hush!" or "Enough already!" Whatever works. It's not always easy. To begin this practice, a lot of energy goes into stopping that voice. It has been in charge for a very long time. The old thought pattern is in a pretty good rut! Those fear thoughts can flow freely until consistently stopped.

As we become more and more fearless, that voice still tries to creep back in, but we can catch it! With practice the fear retreats. There is great inner reward being on the other side of facing fear.

Mantra:

— —— ————— ———— ——
————— ————
——————————

```
C I F F T R A N S M U T E
R A I E S M D I P C V I L
E N G A O G L I R O N T I
E R H R R C I O A N M Y Z
P U T L R O T F C S F S A
C T E E Y N T L T I M T R
O T A S A F L I I S I O D
N E R S B I E G C T S P R
F D B N I D V H E E T P E
R S R E L E O T F N A E W
O W A S I N I I A T K D A
N T I S T C C H C L E C R
T O N N Y E E F E Y I D D
E N C S I T U A T I O N E
```

Ability	Fearlessness	Reward
Brain	Fight	Rutted
Confidence	Flight	Situation
Confront	Little	Sorry
Consistently	Lizard	Stopped
Creep	Mistake	Transmute
Face	Practice	Voice

Commitment

Awaken to a more balanced approach to life by expanding the capacity to hold love in your heart. Heal your loved ones as well as others, including the planet herself. Love, love, love.

Make a stronger commitment to your spiritual path. Accept that your mission may or may not be manifesting itself in physical form at this time. Remain open, holding the intentions of joy, compassion and kindness within. Put one foot in front of the other as Spirit guides. In this way, your mission will become clear. Commit to living your spirituality as a means of service.

Know that you are a teacher in this lifetime, holding spiritual balance on this planet. The new reality and humanity are counting on you.

Mantra:

— —— ——————————— —— ——
——————————————— ———
———————

```
L I F E T I M E B I A O S
M M I S S I O N A H C P E
P C O M C M A A L E S E R
L O I T O I C W A A T N V
A M T E M N C A N L R D I
N P T O M T E K C P O P C
E A M Y I E P E E H N U E
T S C S T N T N H Y G R L
P S L I M T R I E S E P O
T I E U E I A L A I R O V
I O A T N O Y A R C N S E
D N R G T N U I T A D E D
S P I R I T U A L L A N C
E H U M A N I T Y F O O T
```

Accept	Heal	Open
Awaken	Heart	Physical
Balance	Humanity	Planet
Clear	Intention	Purpose
Commitment	Lifetime	Service
Compassion	Loved	Spiritual
Foot	Mission	Stronger

7 Power

A significant leap forward is coming in our development. It is the profound learning of becoming responsible for our own power.

So determined to avoid the negative use of power, many refuse to let their power out at all. They stay in the background lamenting the abuse of power by others.

Higher wisdom is saying that our power to generate a life enhancing vision is expanding. Take a look at what gives power its charge, positive or negative. Remember that the highest power is that which creates love in all its forms.

Commit to lead with love and compassion. Go for what you really want to contribute in life. It's time!

Mantra:

— —— — ——————— —————
———————— ——— ———
————————— — ————
————————— ——————

```
I A M C O N T R I B U T E A
P L A M E N T I N G O A W E
G E N E R A T E R R C V F U
L W B V L N E I E P H O N G
R I G I O E E N S O A I C C
E S L S V G E R P S R D R O
F D E I E A A T O I G H E M
U O A O I T N G N T E I A M
S M R N A I N D S I E G T I
E X N P A V N D I V I H E T
N G I A L E I F B E E E S E
N H N L E A D A L N C R I N
G V G L E A P I E P O W E R
S C O M P A S S I O N I O N
```

Avoid	Higher	Positive
Charge	Lamenting	Power
Commit	Lead	Refuse
Compassion	Leap	Responsible
Contribute	Learning	Vision
Creates	Love	Wisdom
Generate	Negative	

8   **Ambition**

What is ambition? It's a word that has a lot of charge on it. The only thing wrong with ambition is when there is no integrity or responsibility coupled with it.

Being straightforward about goals and aspirations is a good thing. Some of the most respected and loved leaders on this planet are sincere in their commitment to achieve their goals, their ambition, with integrity. Be specific about ambitions. Be more public about the goals and accomplishments you are committed to achieving. Being more public means whatever is appropriate, from sharing with a couple of friends who can help support you, all the way to radio, TV, the whole world…whatever suits your ambition!

Choose a goal, or several. Make sure they excite you! Make sure there is emotion (energy in motion) behind what it is you want to commit to. Get ambitious. Share your ambitions more openly and with a wider group of people. Let others support you in your ambition.

Mantra:

— ————— ——— ————— ——
—— ————————— ————
—————————

—————————— ———

———————————— ———
———— ——— ——— ————— ——

```
S H A R E S U P P O R T W I W
F I I N T E G R I T Y P I N O
D A N S I N C E R E D U D E R
S T A A L N D I N A C B E X L
M Y A M E M B I T S O L R C D
I O N B A W I T R P M I E I H
I N T I D E G R E I M C N T O
I T Y T E C O M S R I M E E P
I T M I R E N T P A T A R N E
D R E O S S P O E T N S G I N
B I L N I T Y A C I N D Y L L
O V E S F O R A T O L L T H Y
A A C H I E V E E N G O A L S
F R I E N D S T D S L O V E D
I S E M O T I O N C H O O S E
```

Achieve	Excite	Public
Ambitions	Friends	Respected
Aspirations	Goals	Share
Choose	Integrity	Sincere
Commit	Leaders	Support
Emotion	Loved	Wider
Energy	Openly	World

9 Synchronicity

There are no such things as accidents or coincidences. Synchronicity is always part of the Divine Plan. We may not know what the accident or coincidence means at the time. Synchronicity demonstrates a level of Oneness, the foundation of the emerging new world.

All things work together for good. Trust that you are putting your energy together with others. Focus on, and take advantage of the synchronicity of events in your life. Whether our human brains or emotions can see it or feel it, or not, "It's all good!"

There is so much happening on the physical level right now, to our friends, our families, acquaintances and business relations. It is a time of great transition for everyone. It is important to continue to stay aware and alert. Trust each happening, each opening, each opportunity, as a part of personal process and spiritual awakening guided by your soul and your soul family.

Mantra:

— — —   — — — — — — —
— — — —   — — —   — —   — — — — —
— — —

```
I A M P T H C R F U T S G
F O T R E U O I O N R G O
O N F O M M I E U O U V O
C E A C E A N F N P S E D
U N M E R N C R D E T M T
S E I S G E I I A N R O O
Y S L S I D D E T I A T G
Y S Y I N N E N I N E I E
S O U L G V N D O G E O T
B R A I N S C S N R Y N H
E N E R G Y E P L A N S E
N O W A C C I D E N T S R
W A T R A N S I T I O N Y
```

Accidents	Focus	Opening
Brains	Foundation	Plan
Coincidence	Friends	Process
Emerging	Good	Soul
Emotions	Human	Together
Energy	Now	Transition
Family	Oneness	Trust

Play

This is a great time to play! Life is amazing. Have fun, play games, and make up some stuff. Lighten up and acknowledge that the world is our playground. Laugh, love and relax. Enjoy!

Unleash imagination. Indulge fanciful stories. Let fantastic visions run wild! Happiness comes when we recreate ourselves with the help of the inner child.

Take the pressure off. Act spontaneously! You may cause disruptions in the status quo. Doing so can bring about new awakenings. Enjoy the journey of life because the journey *is* life. Live it joyously and fully!

Mantra:

— — — — — — — — — — — — — — — — —
— — — — — — — — — —

```
I R E P V I S I O N S C R
E R L R A T C H I L D I E
L E O E I N N E R E F M M
I L V S L A U G H N A A H
G A E S P W I L L J N G A
H X Y U L W I L D O C I P
T S E R A L F B Y Y I N P
E R E E Y G A M E S F A I
N C J O Y O U S L Y U T N
R J O U R N E Y E A L I E
F A N T A S T I C T I O S
D I S R U P T I O N S N S
L I F E O U N L E A S H N
```

Child	Inner	Pressure
Disruptions	Journey	Relax
Enjoy	Joyously	Unleash
Fanciful	Laugh	Visions
Fantastic	Life	Wild
Games	Lighten	Will
Happiness	Love	
Imagination	Play	

The Yoga of Mantra

We have all done mantras at various times in our lives. Singing the alphabet song over and over as youngsters is an example of the power of repeated sounds in action. With countless repetitions of that catchy tune, the ABC mantra worked its magic and embedded the alphabet into our psyche.

The Sanskrit word *mantra* can be broken down into two parts: "man," which means *mind*, and "tra," which means *instrument*. Holy seekers worldwide have known of this powerful instrument of the mind for eons. Prayer beads and rosaries mark each devoted recitation, bringing the divine closer by transcending daily mind chatter.

Through mantras, we have the opportunity to practice yoga. It has been said that in yoga, *asanas* are postures of the body and mantras are postures of the mind. Our Oracle mantras are a blend of ancient mantras and modern positive affirmations.

The positive affirmation technique (an early form of neuro-linguistic programming) was developed by University of California, Santa Cruz, neuroscientists John Grinder and Richard Bandler in the 1970s. It blends psychotherapy and linguistics in order to intentionally rewire mental circuits.

These deeply imprinted thought patterns are the basis of our belief systems. We tend to automatically respond from our entrenched beliefs which impact every choice, thought, or action.

When we want to make a permanent change in our lives, like shifting the perception from the glass is half empty to the glass is half full, we need to modify our thought patterns. Mantras are a great tool to deliberately do that reprogramming. They help keep us connected to an empowering state of mind. As in yoga, the more dedicated the practice, the faster the transformation will take place.

In the beginning was the Word...
-John 1:1

In both Eastern and Western esoteric spiritual traditions, it is believed that the power of words influences our subtle energy bodies, also known as the biofield. Mantras, expressed both aloud and silently, help direct the healing power of our life force energy, *prana*. Mantras can be used to access higher consciousness. From a physics standpoint, that means the sounds themselves can resonate in different parts of the body and mind, creating space for healing and positive changes.

The vibrations of these words, when used aloud with intention, can beneficially impact our perceptions or circumstances. When recited silently, mantras can help us shift. Out with the old unwanted, outgrown, and detrimental default subconscious programming! In with the new paradigm! Mindfulness. Joy. Healthy habits. Loving kindness. We get to choose!

The yoga practice of mantra can enhance both our inner and outer worlds. Awareness of our bodies, minds and spirits can deepen. We consciously change our lives for the better by enriching our minds and belief systems.

Greater understanding of our unique beauty and purpose may be brought to light, helping us to become better every day.

All this and fun puzzles too!

11   Inspiration

It is time to be inspired! Stay aware and alert. What is coming into your space? How do you feel about it? Inspiration is a state of mind.

Inspiration brings pleasure. How can you inspire yourself and others? Invite inspiration in. Remind yourself of the power you have to be inspired. It isn't difficult; it's as easy as breathing. That is just what inspire means, to breathe in.

The best way to be inspired is to express the sincere intention to be inspired. Be inspired by ordinary acts of kindness. Yours or others. Be aware of these opportunities to be inspired. Keep your eyes wide open. Notice those moments when inspiration strikes!

Mantra:

— ————— —— ——
————————— ——— — ——
———————— ———— ——
———————— —————— —————
——— ———

```
I N I N O R D I N A R Y T E
N D O M I N D P O W E R T O
B E I T N S P S T A T E I R
A E D A I N F E E L D I E A
M W F I N C D W I D E I A M
N G A I N T E N T I O N S O
W A Y R K B R E A T H E Y M
S T O I E I E X P R E S S E
N A C T S I N S P I R E S N
S T R I K E S D P A I R E T
M Y I N V I T E N S L E L S
D I F F I C U L T E Y E S F
A O P E N L P L E A S U R E
O O T H E R S P A C E S N T
G T H E S I N C E R E W A Y
```

Acts	Inspire	Others
Alert	Intention	Pleasure
Aware	Invite	Power
Breathe	Kindness	Sincere
Difficult	Mind	Space
Easy	Moments	State
Express	Notice	Strikes
Eyes	Open	Wide
Feel	Ordinary	

Stillness

Deeply realize the present moment. Stop the mind for a few minutes. Listen to the stillness that underlies everything. In listening to that stillness, bring up basic joy, that feeling of gratitude. Give thanks for everything in life. The good, bad, ugly and whatever it is, you have brought it forth for your evolutionary journey.

In the stillness, bless it all.

Close your eyes and say to yourself, "I am so happy! I am so blessed! I am so very thankful for life!" Feel it. Know it. Believe it. Encourage yourself to touch the stillness often as you walk your sacred path.

Make the now, make the stillness, your primary focus. It will hold you up and get you through.

Mantra:

— —— —————— ——— ———
—— —— ————— —— —————
————— ——— —————————
——— ———— ———— ————
——— ———

```
S T I L L N E S S D E E P L Y
P R E S E N T R E A L I Z E I
A M T A O U P R I M A R Y C H
I N G C T H E J S T O P O B Y
O F M R Y G R A T I T U D E B
E I N E J O U R N E Y U H L G
B Y B D C L O S E E I N A I N
G S T O U C H F E E L D P E P
T I L E N C O U R A G E P V R
L A N D S M O M E N T R Y E O
H T H A N K F U L W A L K U C
T T I N G L I S T E N I T H E
E M I N D B L E S S D E O W S
N J F O C U S K N O W S U S S
T F O P A T H R N O L I F E W
```

Believe	Journey	Realize
Bless	Know	Sacred
Close	Life	Stillness
Deeply	Listen	Stop
Encourage	Moment	Thankful
Feel	Path	Touch
Focus	Present	Underlies
Gratitude	Primary	Walk
Happy	Process	

Connection

Opportunities to connect are being offered. Part of the energy of connection is walking the path with an open, broad view of everything. Be alert to the surroundings, and available for connection, without fear, yet with discernment. Whatever you are connecting with at the moment, know, without judgment, that this is either right for you or not.

Feel that connection to the right choice at the right time. Focus on being connected with the people, places and things you want in your life. Connect to what you choose to finish, purge, or eliminate with love, whatever it is.

Openness and connectedness to all living things will bring us more and more to the life we want. We are connected to this new reality. We integrate new ways of looking at the world and all that is.

Mantra:

— —— —————————— —— ——
—————— ——————— ——— —
——— —— ———— —— ——
—————

```
D I S C E R N M E N T A I A
W M C O P E N N E S S V O N
N A E L O O K I N G C A T I
N G L T E N E R G Y V I E W
F E O K P L A C E S M L Y D
F O L I I B R O A D P A T H
R E C I V N R I G H T B I N
F E E U M E G E W O R L D S
S I A L S I E C O N N E C T
N C N L E A N C H O O S E N
D A L I I L I A P E O P L E
L O V E S T S W T H I N G S
E L L I N H Y A L E R T M Y
W O R I N T E G R A T E L D
```

Alert	Feel	People
Available	Finish	Places
Broad	Focus	Reality
Choose	Integrate	Right
Connect	Looking	Things
Discernment	Love	View
Eliminate	Openness	Walking
Energy	Path	World

14   Courage

Things are changing and courage is needed. There are two types of courage. Physical courage stands up in the face of threat, hardship, pain or death. Moral courage facilitates right action in the face of unpopular attitudes, opposition, shame, scandal or distress.

Have the courage to walk your own path, to be a spiritual warrior and face your fears. Do what needs to be done. Hold on to the truth that really All is Well.

Everything is changing! Be focused and stand tall in the truth of who you are. There is plenty of fear, chaos and concern. Everything has to be dealt with in daily life, including money, the future, our livelihoods, the state of the global economy, families, children, and so much more. Change is the only constant in the universe; it is the scariest thing for humans to deal with. These transformational times are really an opportunity to pull our courage to the forefront.

Mantra:

—   — — — —   — — —   — — — — — — —   — —
— — — —   — —   — — — —   — —   — — — — —
— —   — —   — — — — —   — — —   — —   — —
— — —   —   — —

```
I F A M I L Y M O N E Y H A V
T E T H S P I R I T U A L E C
O H P A T H F U T U R E U R A
M O R A L P H Y S I C A L U G
E T O E O P P O S I T I O N W
A L K H A R D S H I P E M P W
F E A R D T Y P A C A C C O A
U N I V E R S E C H T O O P R
C S H T A O S T T A A N U U R
N H H D T A L L I N I O R L I
N M A A H Y T R O G U M A A O
T H A O M N D T N E O Y G R R
B E W H S E C H I L D R E N O
R I G H T S C A N D A L I A M
```

Action	Future	Shame
Change	Hardship	Spiritual
Chaos	Money	Tall
Children	Moral	Threat
Courage	Opposition	Universe
Death	Path	Unpopular
Economy	Physical	Warrior
Family	Right	
Fear	Scandal	

Cornerstone

The cornerstone is the person, place, faith, feeling or practice upon which all in our lives is built. In construction, it is the first stone set of a masonry foundation, important since all other stones will be set in reference to this stone. Think about your cornerstone now. Do you have one?

The foundations of our lives tend to be our core beliefs, philosophies, and principles upon which we see and relate to the world. Generally, they were passed on to us by our parents, our society, our culture and our peers.

Occasionally these foundations may shift or even crash. These can be times of great breakthroughs and cleansings, asking us to establish new cornerstones, new thoughts and ideas about who we are and how we see ourselves.

A new level of consciousness is arriving. Examine your cornerstone. Decide if it is still the solid foundation upon which to build. Know at the heart level that you have been brought to this time to establish the cornerstone of who you are now.

Mantra:

— —— —————————— ————
—— —————————— ———
———————— —— ——
——————— ——
————————— —— —— —— —
————— —— ——— ————————

```
C O N S C I O U S N E S S I A
M B M E D I S O L I D T A T I
P E R S O N N G U P O N M Y C
O R N E S T A B L I S H E R R
S T C R A S H P R A C T I C E
O N E A N K D M A S O N R Y A
C H S H I F T A N G N I N G L
I T O R F L O H W I S N G M I
Y F H C O R N E R S T O N E T
G D E C I D E R C O R E A T Y
P I A E T U D X E B U I L D T
L O R I L I D E A S C G T A S
A E T F A I T H I M T B H U I
C L V F O U N D A T I O N D M
E P E E R S Y G N E O N W R E
A L I C L E A N S I N G E T Y
```

Breakthrough	Establish	Peers
Build	Examine	Person
Cleansing	Faith	Place
Consciousness	Feeling	Practice
Construction	Foundation	Reality
Core	Heart	Shift
Cornerstone	Ideas	Solid
Crash	Level	
Decide	Masonry	

16   The Shift

A shift is taking place on our planet. Please believe and hold space for non-violence. Stay real and true to who you are. Deception and lack of integrity seem to be on the rise. With the world in so much chaos, it is more important than ever to pay attention to what is right in front of us. Not yesterday. Not tomorrow. Right now.

The world is shifting to a new reality. We are here to help birth it. Do not resist any forced changes in life. It is through these transitions that we will find ourselves in a totally new place. A new level of consciousness, a new feeling level is rising. A new perspective prepares for the energies that are to come. Some of these experiences are difficult, sad, and hard to believe. They can be brilliant, happy, and fulfilling too. Take it all in stride.

Be at peace. Work on releasing old ways of being. Be willing to break old patterns. Be the change you want to see in the world!

Mantra:

— —— —————————— ————

——— ——— ———————— ——

—— —— ——

```
C R I P L A N E T C H A O S A
H E F P O S I T I O N W O R K
A L M U A C C E P T A N C E S
N E H A L P R E P A R E T I P
G A F T T F S T R I D E R I A
E S I N G T I B I R T H A M T
P E A C E W E L I T H T N P T
B E L I E V E N L H E N S O E
E P E R S P E C T I V E I R R
W R E A L I T Y R I N E T T N
A L W I L L I N G I O G I A S
I N T E G R I T Y T Y N O N B
H A P P Y B R I L L I A N T R
C O N S C I O U S N E S S T E
S H I F T D E C E P T I O N A
O C O M E D I F F I C U L T K
```

Acceptance	Difficult	Prepare
Attention	Fulfilling	Reality
Believe	Happy	Release
Birth	Important	Shift
Break	Integrity	Stride
Brilliant	Patterns	Transitions
Change	Peace	Willing
Chaos	Perspective	Work
Consciousness	Planet	
Deception	Position	

17   Mother-Deep

Your being is as ancient as the beginning of things. It is that which endures forever. Once in touch with it, you are in touch with what Lao-Tzu calls the Mother-Deep.

The mother nature of Tao is eternal. It is the great cooperative process by which all is created, and all is taken care of. The rain falls out of the sky and the earth gathers it up. From the heights of the earth, water flows down to the ocean. From the ocean, waters rise, become clouds and move to the shore. The endless process that continuously gives birth to itself is the source of all creation. This is Mother-Deep.

In the great flowing rivers and the smallest trickling streams we see the motion of Mother-Deep. In the skies, in the earth, the Mother-Deep is always changing. Nourishing. Eroding. Moving. Creating. The spirit of Mother-Deep regenerates endlessly. It has no beginning; it has no end.

Look at life around you. The motion of Mother-Deep is everywhere. It is the origin of everything. Allow yourself to flow with it.

Mantra:

— —————— —— ———— ———
———— —— —————————
———— ————— —— ——— ———
——————— —————————
——————

```
S  I  E  A  S  I  L  E  T  E  R  N  A  L  Y
G  T  E  O  W  I  R  I  V  E  R  T  T  H  T
H  E  R  A  N  C  I  E  N  T  F  L  R  O  W
O  F  E  E  R  V  O  C  E  A  N  E  I  R  Y
T  H  I  N  A  T  F  L  O  W  G  T  C  H  A
T  C  O  M  E  M  H  R  A  I  N  S  K  M  Y
C  R  E  A  T  I  O  N  W  A  Y  A  L  N  D
T  H  N  O  U  R  I  S  H  I  N  G  I  E  P
S  R  E  B  Y  R  C  H  A  N  G  I  N  G  R
K  R  E  G  E  N  E  R  A  T  E  S  G  E  O
I  G  E  N  E  R  M  O  T  I  O  N  A  T  C
E  E  E  R  O  D  I  N  G  N  A  T  U  R  E
S  M  M  O  T  H  E  R  S  P  I  R  I  T  S
Y  S  E  L  C  O  N  T  I  N  U  O  U  S  S
C  O  O  P  E  R  A  T  I  V  E  D  E  E  P
F  E  N  D  L  E  S  S  L  Y  A  L  L  O  W
```

Allow	Eroding	Rain
Ancient	Eternal	Regenerates
Changing	Flow	River
Continuous	Mother	Skies
Cooperative	Motion	Spirit
Creation	Nature	Stream
Deep	Nourishing	Trickling
Earth	Ocean	
Endlessly	Process	

Imagination

Rely on imaginative power to address whatever situation is taking place.

Throw the analytical mind to the wind. Entertain that you are, indeed, the ruler of an incredible universe. Yours! Open yourself to an amazing fountain of possibility. Go on. Imagine how it could be!

As always with our growth potential, we have to let go of our limiting beliefs. Step into the ability to willingly not know the answer. Let it be revealed through imagination – there are no mistakes with imagination…let it run wild, let your dreams flow.

Mantra:

— — — — — — — — —

— — — — — — — — — — — — — — —

— — — — — — — — — — — — — —

— — — — — — — — — — — — — —

— — — — — — — — — — — — — —

```
W I A A I M A G I N E L L W O
W I M M A N S W E R Y I M I A
G I N N A A C P L A C E T L I
W I L D O Z N R T S T E P L O
P R U N F R I E E E A N D I L
O G D E T G O N O D F M Y N L
S R R I M I E U G T I I R G N
S O E G B E L N N I E B U L P
I W A A N A L Y T I C A L Y O
B T M F M I N D S E V A E E W
I H S A D D R E S S R E R B E
L O P O T E N T I A L T R O R
I P U T F O U N T A I N A S T
T E H E M I S T A K E S W I E
Y N A Y I S I T U A T I O N N
T I F L O W R E V E A L E D S
```

Address	Imagine	Revealed
Amazing	Incredible	Ruler
Analytical	Mind	Situation
Answer	Mistakes	Step
Dreams	Open	Universe
Entertain	Place	Wild
Flow	Possibility	Willingly
Fountain	Potential	Wind
Growth	Power	

19   Truth

There are different schools of thought as to whether truth, with a capital T, is absolute or relative. Regardless, make sure to tell the truth. Stand in the truth. Be your true self.

Some believe that it is all right not to be truthful. Spin doctoring has become a way of life in our global community. Speaking your truth, though sometimes very hard, provides great release and re-energization. Say it. Own it. Do not spin what you believe or feel is the Truth.

Truth may be different for another person. Many so-called facts or *the way it is* are really matters of perception and opinion. It takes compassionate understanding to know what truth is for you. Expressing and standing in that truth while allowing others to express and stand in theirs is on the road to true mastery.

Each of us is a sovereign being. We evolve and grow at our own rates of vibration. We each have our individual truths. Meditate on Truth. Express your Truth!

Mantra:

— — — — — — — — —
— — — — — — — — — — — — — —
— — — — — — — — — — — — — — — — —
— — — — — — — — — — — —
— — — — — — — — — — —

```
I A S M O B E L I E V E P E S
P N A P T O R O P I N I O N P
E E V B E R E L E A S E C E I
R I I E S A V C R E A T E E N
C A B X L O K L L E D V E L S
E O R P F A L I E V O L V E I
P F A A T A L U N R C U T H N
T A T N N D C L T G T T O M D
I A I D L L O T O E O W M A I
O Y O T R U T H S W R T R S V
N U N E S O V E R E I G N T I
S E L G R O W I N G N N F E D
T E X P R E S S I N G O G R U
M E D I T A T E N G A G E Y A
E X P R E L A T I V E R E S L
S I T S E L S T A N D I N G F
```

Absolute	Expressing	Relative
Allowing	Facts	Release
Believe	Growing	Sovereign
Create	Individual	Speaking
Doctoring	Mastery	Spin
Engage	Meditate	Standing
Evolve	Opinion	Truth
Expand	Perception	Vibration

Desire

Allow your inner child to come out and have some fun!
Whee!! I'm ready. Are you??

Spontaneity and enjoyment of life need to be expressed. More
than likely, you have been busy with lots of things, meeting
the needs of family, friends and others. Remember how
important laughter, joy and temporary freedom from
responsibility is. Engage it now. Enjoy a little rejuvenation.

As you travel along your path, it is important to take time to
relax and rebalance your life. Rekindle your desire and
passion for living.

Mantra:

— ———— — ——————— ———
—————— —— —————— ————

```
I H A L I V I N G V E R A R
R P A S S T R A V E L E S E
E E X P R E S S E D I B P A
L A U G H T E R O N A A O D
A N R E K I N D L E D L N Y
X E N J O Y I N N E R A T D
R E J U V E N A T I O N A E
I M P O R T A N T S I C N R
E N E E D S T C E W H E E A
L I F E P A T H H N O E I L
N J F R E E D O M I G O T L
T I M E F A M I L Y L A Y O
Y L P A S S I O N I F D G W
E F R I E N D S D E S I R E
```

Allow	Important	Rebalance
Child	Inner	Rejuvenation
Desire	Laughter	Rekindle
Engage	Life	Relax
Enjoy	Living	Spontaneity
Expressed	Needs	Time
Family	Passion	Travel
Freedom	Path	Whee
Friends	Ready	

Why the Eye? The Eyes Have It!

Our eyes are the windows we open to perceive the world. They are our personal internal cameras taking videos of what is happening around us. That nearly real time recording is then shown on the movie screen inside our heads, creating reality as we perceive it. Our eyes are sensitive to a very narrow band of frequencies, the visible light spectrum. There is an enormous range of frequencies in the electromagnetic spectrum; many things are going on in our world that our eyes cannot see.

...The fact that the eye, by its marvelous power,

widens our otherwise very narrow range of perception

far beyond the limits of the small world which is our own,

to embrace myriads of other worlds, suns and stars

in the infinite depths of the universe,

would make it justifiable to assert,

that it is an organ of a higher order...

The saying then, that the soul shows itself in the eye,

is deeply founded and

we feel that it expresses a great truth.

-Nikola Tesla

The eyes are the window to the soul. Often attributed to William Shakespeare, this old English proverb is rich in meaning. When we look into another's eyes, we can somehow see the quality of the light within. In our western culture, it is a gesture of honesty and openness to look directly into the eyes of the person we are communicating with. Or is it communing? We can sometimes get lost in the beauty of the mini-galaxies contained within the irises of our beloved.

Our eyes are as individual as we are. We each have a different structure of lines, dots and colors in our irises. These unique biological signatures are the basis for some current security protocols, where the eye is scanned to allow access to something protected.

Science, both ancient and modern, has proven that the eyes are a window to the soul medically as well as metaphorically. From as far back as 3000 years ago, archaeological data reveals that in Egypt, China and India there was much attention devoted to the study of the iris and its relation to organs of the body.

In ancient Egypt, the eye was utilized as a medical measuring device. Various elements correlated to the senses. The mathematical proportions of the eye were used to calculate proper fractions and accurate amounts of ingredients to compound medicine.

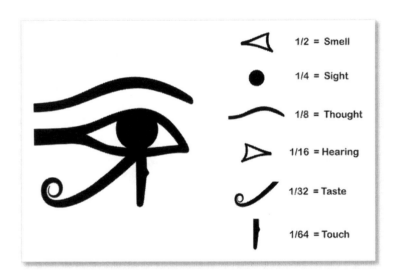

Practitioners of the ancient diagnostic practice of iridology can look at an eye and notice where in the body a disruption or disease process is occurring. Silver plates with detailed iris images were discovered in King Tutankhamun's tomb.

In traditional Tibetan medicine, the condition of the eyes was carefully noted by doctors who related markings to liver functioning and blood disorders. Dr. Ignatz Von Peczely is the Hungarian father of western iridology. After studying the irises of patients before and after surgery, he published his findings in 1867 and later created charts linking regions of the iris to organs in the body.

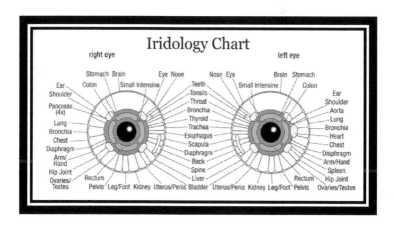

The eye is the lamp of the body.

If your eyes are healthy, your whole body will be full of light.

But if your eyes are unhealthy,

your whole body will be full of darkness.

-Matthew 6:22, 23

21   **Encouragement**

We can change and heal our lives. Many of us feel that we have to face the transformations and challenges alone. Everybody is going through it. There are massive changes of energy here on planet Earth. We already know what we need to pay attention to, heal, or change.

Believe in yourself! Encourage yourself to make these changes. Divinity, Source, your guides, angels and spirits are all pushing power and encouragement your way. Continue meditations and empowering inner work. Love yourself. Trust yourself. Know in your heart that *this too shall pass.* All aspects of life that need change can and will be changed through love.

Practice drawing love in with each breath. Release any unwanted pain or pattern with each exhale. Do it now…

Mantra:

— — — — — — — — — — —
— — — — — — — — — — — — — — —
— — — — — — — — — —

```
T G U I D E S M A S S I V E T
A R I A M R S O U R C E L E S
L L A E A E N E R G Y S O I U
N G L N O I T N E T T A V T R
M N R O S E M P O W E R E S T
E O Y O W F Y D O B Y R E V E
A I T U B L O E B R S G O V E
N T I R I P S R E E N H E A L
I A N M E H E L M E G I A P A
N T I B I A E T L A L N A S H
G I V A T A N L D E T S A P X
F D I H S A A T B T S I E H E
U E D E R H A N G E L S O N C
L M E N C O U R A G E M E N T
A L O N E S P O S I T I V E S
```

Allow	Empower	Meaningful
Alone	Encouragement	Meditation
Angels	Energy	Pass
Attention	Everybody	Positive
Believe	Exhale	Release
Breath	Guides	Source
Challenges	Heal	Spirit
Change	Love	Transformations
Divinity	Massive	Trust

22   **Belief**

It is time to turn old belief structures on their heads! We are in a whole new territory. Our need to be loved, to be appreciated or approved of may be getting in the way of the new choices we need to make. Don't underestimate your abilities because of the old baggage of limiting beliefs.

Take the opportunity of a different perspective on what is happening. Belief structure is our filter of the visible universe. With these changing times, going on both the inside and the outside, we cannot even count on what we used to think was the visible, sustainable world. Faith, gratitude, compassion, love, and connection need to be brought into belief structures in order to clear them. You are wonderful just as are you are right now! Say it aloud, "I am wonderful just as I am right now!"

Focus on the opportunities being offered by spirit to be who you are without affectation or mask. Trust in your connection to the Divine. Go ahead, be yourself! Know that it is perfect!

Mantra:

— —— ————— —— — —————— ——— —————— ———————— —————— ——— —————————— —— ——— —————— —— ——————

```
I A M E C M H E T S D A E H L
D F A D I L N A H L O V T I N
V I S I B L E G G W A I Y B E
I L K S U S T A I N A B L E N
G T D T I T R E R F F C U T L
Y E N U G R L U F R E D N O W
U R F O C U S E I T I L I B A
I D E D I C C A N D L I V A N
E S G R A T I T U D E T E G R
U V C T A U C E D I B B R G Y
Y R O T I R R E T V T T S A H
E Z I L A E R E N I F N E G O
C O M P A S S I O N R U C E E
N S O F I N S I D E O O H E A
T S U R T V P E R F E C T E N
```

Abilities	Filter	Right
Affectation	Focus	Structures
Baggage	Gratitude	Sustainable
Belief	Heads	Territory
Clear	Inside	Trust
Compassion	Love	Universe
Connection	Mask	Visible
Count	Outside	Wonderful
Divine	Perfect	
Faith	Realize	

Awareness

Feeling stuck? Dulled by life or by the challenges you have been experiencing? This Oracle is here to assure you of your path. You are heading in the right direction. Now is the time to awaken your awareness and your spirit. Move on!

Use awareness, that perceptive ability, to get out of whatever it is you are presently feeling trapped in. This is a powerful time of spiritual insight. Learn from past negative experiences.

Your angels and guides are there. Listen to them. Focus your awareness. Feel what is right for you. Break through the limitations. Awaken your spirit completely to who you are. Know above all that God/All That Is/Source is the totality of your living experience. Connect your earthly awareness to this totality. It will encourage enlightenment and further awaken awareness. Greater changes are on the way! Move out of any limitations that are holding you back.

Mantra:

— ————— ——————— ———— —
—————————

——————————— ———

————————— ———— ——

—————— —— —————— —

—————— ——— —————

———— ——— —————— —

```
E I B E L C A R O R E A K T H
R N O Y A U G H P A S I K T N
E G L T I R I P S A T N I V E
E A B I L I T Y B L O S S O M
X P E L G G P H R W S I I E N
L E C A C H A L L E N G E S E
S I V T A T T P N Y N H D E E
M O S O T I H E O N P T A D L
P A I T M N R R N T O O I I A
C C E P E A D C T M W R M U Y
D F I V W N I E N E E E N G A
T O U A R G E P L C R N A N D
M C O N N E C T T L F U T E R
G U E P W L I I K C U T S T H
T S H E E S O V D I L D V S I
N E C H A N G E S N E K A W A
```

Ability	Dulled	Oracle
Angels	Earthly	Path
Assure	Enlightenment	Perceptive
Awaken	Focus	Powerful
Awareness	Guides	Right
Blossom	Insight	Spirit
Challenges	Know	Stuck
Changes	Listen	Totality
Connect	Move	
Direction	Open	

24   Letting Go

Now is a time to focus on letting go. We need to let go with love, with understanding, with compassion and with forgiveness. Release stuff that has kept you tied up for years.

To use the analogy of life as a river, consider that most folks cling to the bank, afraid to let go and risk being carried along by the current of the river. When the pain of hanging on becomes greater than the fear of letting go, we do let go and the river begins to carry us along safely. Relax, with love and trust; look ahead and guide the course. Choose which of the many branches of the river to follow while still going with the flow. Enjoy being here now, flowing with what is. At the same time, guide yourself consciously toward your goals by taking full responsibility for creating your own life.

Release the needy aspects of life that hold you back. Claim your highest self. Struggle is part of being on planet Earth; mental struggle is mitigated by spiritual awareness. Spiritual awareness, consciousness itself, grows as we release and let go of those aspects of ourselves that no longer serve us.

Mantra:

—— — ————— ——— ——— ——
— ———— —————— ——
————— ————

```
F T R U S T C A S I R S R R
L O V E E U E L A M L I E X
O C O U R S E A I A V S N D
W L O R V H E T O E P A K S
S S E N E V I G R O F F S T
G N O I S G C G N F L E I M
T O W T A C L S H I N L R E
L A U T I R I P S E T Y E N
O W E A R B N O R D S T L T
M D E D I U G A U X B T E A
M I A L C Y W H I S A G A L
N O I S S A P M O C N L S H
S T R U G G L E E S K E E T
Y G O O D B R A N C H E S R
G N I D N A T S R E D N U S
```

Awareness	Forgiveness	Responsibility
Bank	Goals	Risk
Branches	Guide	River
Claim	Highest	Safely
Cling	Letting	Serve
Compassion	Love	Spiritual
Consciousness	Mental	Struggle
Course	Mitigated	Trust
Current	Relax	Understanding
Flow	Release	

Growth

Experience growth that considers all aspects of your being.

Do not resist the challenges that come with growth. No matter what is going on, inside your head or out there in your environment, check it out. At the heart level, know that your new story, the path you consider embarking on will support your continuous development and bring health and vitality.

You are poised for an exciting time that will lead to greater success and happiness. Familiar habits are generally threatened when growth opportunities are up. Go ahead. Step into the unknown. Trust that these steps will support this huge leap in development. Are you ready?

Mantra:

— —— ———————— ——
————————— ———— — ——
——— ———— — ——— ———————

```
I L A M D Y T I L A T I V T
W T E I E M B A R K I N G
L R L V V B A L A N C E I S
D O U N E T R A E H M L D T
E P N G L L A T O N E L S E
S P K S O A I S O A R H U P
I U N C P R L R P O D E C I
O S O F M R I R W E I A C C
P T W U E V M E E W C L E H
A R N S N H A D T I A T S H
M U I E T I F I F O R H S W
H S A W T I T S T I B A H C
T T O A S S E N I P P A H N
B R E N N I E O O U T E R C
G N I E B O M C K C E H C E
```

Aspects	Growth	Poised
Balance	Habits	Resist
Being	Happiness	Step
Check	Head	Success
Consider	Health	Support
Continuous	Heart	Trust
Development	Inner	Unknown
Embarking	Leap	Vitality
Environment	Level	Worlds
Familiar	Outer	

Possibility

Step outside of yourself, away from the way you think about things, away from your patterns of thought. See the beginnings of your new story. Things are changing up fast, daily it seems. Focus on innovating possibility in your life!

Follow through on changes that have been taking place within you. Begin to identify and nail down a few of the possibilities you have been considering. Move them from a possibility into an opportunity. You can do it. Your life has been leading up to this. Know in your heart that all the energies flowing now are pointing you in the direction of something new.

So much has been going on! Take time to meditate on the possibilities that Spirit has placed in front of you. New energy is coming in to support you in these immense changes. Lots of folks are having physical reactions to these new energies. Be centered. Meditate and work on life mastery tools. Stay calm, cool and collected. Stay in the present moment. There are so many more possibilities coming your way!

Mantra:

— —— ——————————— ———
————————— ——————————— ——
—————— ————— —— ———
—————

```
I Y R O T S A M V I S I O D N
Y T I N U T R O P P O I N E G
L I M M E N S E T N E S E R P
O L E F I L M E D I T A T E A
O I N A I L N D T H E A R T H
C B E T H G U O H T E R E N R
B I R S Y E N C O U R A G E E
C S G N I N N I G E B R E C A
A S I R T I D E T C E L L O C
N O E E G N I G N A H C G T T
M P S T Y F U T U R V E O W I
Y R E T S A M T N E M O M I O
T L E A D I N G C A L M N H N
M Y N P L A C E E S W S T N S
O R Y D A I L Y F I T N E D I
```

Beginnings	Identify	Patterns
Calm	Immense	Place
Centered	Innovating	Possibility
Changing	Leading	Present
Collected	Life	Reactions
Cool	Mastery	Story
Daily	Meditate	Thought
Encourage	Moment	Tools
Energies	Nail	
Heart	Opportunity	

27 Willpower

Commit to a deeper level of discipline with regard to time engaged in spiritual practices. Willpower is about commitment and discipline. Take up the challenge! Make sure you are spending your precious time wisely.

This discipline brings the power of our angels, guides and spirits, to deepen our relationship with self and Divinity. Create your altar. Have your fire ceremonies. Write your intentions. Enjoy your space, time alone to meditate, listen, chant, drum and dance. Stay out of your mind; touch the stillness within. Expand your inner center of spirit; connect with Source.

Willpower will bring loving, compassionate and free spirit into daily life, activities and experiences.

Mantra:

— — — — — — — — — — — — — — —
— — — — — — — — — — — — — — —
— — — — — — — — — — — — —
— — — — — —

```
R C I R S U O I C E R P A E M
E C O O E T M Y M I T T N E D
N T E M C P I O L B E O I E R
N N X N P E E L G E L A N L E
I C P O O A R E L A S I V C T
H O A N I I S E D N L I N T N
C M N N E R T S M P E A W N E
U M D G A T Y N I O D S A A C
O I N T F L S C E O N D S H E
T T L L I C S I O T N I M C N
P A O A A I S S L I N A E O G
N W D A D S O U R C E I T S A
T P R A C T I C E S F R E E G
S P I R I T U A L D R U M E E
P E R S O W I L L P O W E R N
```

Alone	Deeper	Listen
Altar	Discipline	Practices
Center	Drum	Precious
Ceremonies	Engage	Source
Chant	Expand	Spiritual
Commit	Flow	Stillness
Compassionate	Free	Touch
Daily	Inner	Willpower
Dance	Intention	Wisely

Compassion

There is chaos in our nations, our religions, our families, our planet and our very own personal and professional lives. Now is the time for compassionate understanding.

Go deeper within. Find nourishment in writings, prayers and meditations. Courageously continue this journey of opening the heart and soul.

The Buddha said everyone is suffering in some way. Hinduism says we are ignorant of our union with God. Islam says we suffer from forgetfulness; we forget Allah and act ungodly. Christianity says we are inherently sinful, but may be redeemed. Judaism says we develop the capacity for evil and good over time. Each religion seeks to answer the human questions. Pick the one that suits you. If no religion calls, ask Spirit for help. Pray and meditate for guidance. Have a compassionate heart for your own situation.

Carry the healing spirit of compassion. Be open to helping all, including yourself. Commit with unconditional love to others and yourself. Become whole. Be gentle. Be patient. Be tolerant. Be understanding. Help others help themselves with love surrounding each step. Compassion is not a sentiment; it is the ultimate and most meaningful energetic embodiment of spiritual and emotional maturity.

Mantra:

— _ _ _ _ _ _ _ _ _ _ _ _ _ _ _ _ _ _
_ _ _ _ _ _ _ _ _ _ _ _ _ _ _
_ _ _ _ _ _ _ _ _ _ _ _
_ _ _ _ _ _ _ _ _
_ _ _ _ _ _ _ _ _ _ _ _ _

```
I N F R S T O L E R A N T U E
A Q E E R R E L I G I O N N L
E S U P S S E S L Y O N E D P
E N P E O N O W S M O Y M E H
E A A E S A O P S I R M H R T
A N T D H T I I S N S D S S S
H A I C H R I S T I A N I T Y
R G E E I M A O U A Y L R A T
O V N T E P W D N I N T U N I
H W T I M P N A M S G L O D R
L H I O R I G E N S N C N I U
O O C A H E M B O D I M E N T
U L Y T N N F T I S L A M G A
E E I T R U N F C O A N D D M
R W L I A H D D U B E T I U O
N E V O L A L L Y S H E L P J
```

Answers	Hinduism	Questions
Buddha	Islam	Religion
Chaos	Judaism	Spirit
Christianity	Love	Suffering
Compassion	Maturity	Tolerant
Deeper	Nations	Understanding
Embodiment	Nourishment	Whole
Gentle	Open	Within
Healing	Patient	
Help	Prayer	

Cooperation

Cooperation is the process of working or acting together for a common purpose. Living cooperatively means to suspend judgment, cultural values and intolerance. Everyone is suffering in some way. There is no need to decide what is right for another. Everyone is on their own soul journey.

Cooperation removes blocks and promotes spiritual alignment. Old feelings, abandonment, abuse, neglect and loss are overcome. Emerge more fully into life. Pay attention to the relationships between body, mind and spirit. Facilitate deeper cooperation on the inside. Open consciousness to cooperation on all levels. It will improve attitude, confidence and awareness, and thereby broaden the scope of transformation.

To cooperate both inwardly and outwardly is to further embody and emanate Divine Essence. Be who you are! Respect the sovereignty and decisions of others.

Mantra:

— —— ————————————
———— —————— ———
—————— —— — ——— —————
—— ——————

```
I E S S E N C E V O R P M I A
C M C S O D Y O O D I V I N E
E O P E E U U L R A T I N T C
G G O W T C L T D I T H A M N
J E R P N Y O N I R S N E L E
U M E E S F R O T A A N C D
D O T D M R S O P M T W N T I
G C A T N E A E D M A T H F
E R T O G E R T N S R O S U N
M E I G I N I I E O A C N O
E V L E L E M W L O R P S T C
N O I T A M R O F S N A R T A
T G C H E O T I R I P S W U F
G R A E G N I R E F F U S A P
O W F R I N W A R D L Y D O B
T H T C E P S E R V A L U E S
```

Alignment	Essence	Purpose
Attitude	Facilitate	Respect
Awareness	Improve	Soul
Body	Intolerance	Spirit
Common	Inwardly	Suffering
Confidence	Judgement	Together
Cooperation	Mind	Transformation
Divine	Outwardly	Values
Emanate	Overcome	
Emerge	Process	

Love

You are truly loved, more than you can imagine. Feel it! Allow it to flow into your heart chakra, and out into All That Is. Love, love, love! You are merging more and more with your Divine Essence. Identify and understand that you are not required to be all things to all people. You have all the time you need to do what you need to do. You attract everything you need no matter what is going on.

Loving yourself is life affirming. Loving what you do provides great balance. Loving others, being kind, being compassionate, being supportive, being love, provides the planet with an immeasurable sense of wellness and beauty. Focus on love. We are beginning a whole new story, a whole new culture, a whole new civilization. You are part of it, wherever you are. Begin with love. Trust Spirit in all things, even what you resist. Trust your purpose. Love is the answer.

Mantra:

— — — — — —   — — — —   — — —   — — — —

```
E A I D N A T S R E D N U P
R L F T S U R T V M C T Y U
U L B F D I V I N E H C F R
T O L A I O T M V R A A I P
L W E F R R A E N G K R T O
U F L D O U M S C I R T N S
C O M P A S S I O N A T E E
W C P F E E L A N G A A D N
I U E C N E S S E G L L I S
S S P L A N E T A M K O A E
M L L O T S I S E R M I V B
R E W S N A V I M A G I N E
W H E A R T E B E A U T Y D
```

Affirming	Essence	Merging
Allow	Feel	Planet
Answer	Flow	Purpose
Attract	Focus	Resist
Balance	Heart	Sense
Beauty	Identify	Supportive
Chakra	Imagine	Time
Compassionate	Immeasurable	Trust
Culture	Kind	Understand
Divine	Love	Wellness

The Eyes of Horus

The symbolic eye on our cover comes from ancient Egypt. It is known as the Eye of Horus. In Egyptian mythology, the sun and the moon were regarded as the eyes of the great falcon sky god Horus. It was said that the sun was his right eye and the moon his left. They traversed the sky when Horus flew across it.

The left eye, the Eye of Thoth, is the symbol of the moon. It reflects fluid, feminine, mystical energy, and supports intuition and oracles. The right Eye of Ra represents the sun. It emanates logical, masculine, magical energy, and rules reason and mathematics.

82

Together, the eyes represent the whole of the universe, a concept similar to the yin-yang.

A well-known myth describes a battle between Horus and his uncle, Set. Horus' left eye was torn out. The god Thoth restored his eye, at which point it was given the name Wadjet, meaning whole or healthy. Since the left eye was involved, this story relates to the monthly waxing and waning of the moon during which the moon appears to have been torn out of the sky before being restored.

The Wadjet became a powerful symbol of protection, which has been passed down through millennia. Now both eyes are generally referred to as the Eye of Horus. The design is still fashionable in jewelry, treasure boxes and artwork. It is believed to ensure safety and health, as well as cultivate wisdom and prosperity.

The Eye of Providence is a visual we see almost daily. It continues the tradition of the single eye as a symbol of protection and divine favor. Known also as the All-Seeing Eye of God, the single eye is usually enclosed in a triangle (representing the Christian trinity) and often surrounded by rays of light. It represents the eye of God watching over humankind.

The Eye of Providence appears on the United States one dollar bill as a part of the Great Seal of the United States. In 1782, William Barton, consultant and artist on the third Great Seal committee, suggested the eye and the pyramid as part of the design. The pyramid symbolizes strength and duration. The motto above the Eye, *Annuit Cœptis,* borrowed from the Roman poet Virgil, means *favor our undertakings.*

The eye, the pyramid, and the motto combined may be said to mean, *God in your omniscience, please watch over us and favor our undertakings. Please give us the strength to endure.* When giving or receiving a one dollar bill, consider this mantra.

God, (Spirit, Source, The Divine by the Name You Choose...)
Please watch over us and favor our undertakings.
We accept the strength to endure, thrive, and enjoy.
Thank you.

We choose what we embed into our consciousness. Let's make it something that supports our highest good!

Expression

Unleash your limitations! Express who you truly are. Spirit is awakening. Be vulnerable enough to express these changes. Allow yourself to face your fears, and do it anyway.

Your unique insight and perceptions are true gifts from Spirit. You truly are in healing service to this planet and all living things.

There is great confidence that is obtained by expressing without affectation or expectation. Express YOU! Truly! You, and all living things, are unique expressions of Divine Love. Your inner voice can speak out into the world, sharing feelings that grow from your unlimited spiritual reality. Express your love, joy, kindness, compassion and heartfelt empathy. It is all part of who you are. Expression is healing and rewarding. Expand it more and more.

Mantra:

__ __ ____ __ _____
___ _____ __ _____
___ _____
_____ ____ ____
_____ _

```
E M P A T H Y I A M O U P E S
U N E V O L P E X P A N D T T
Q O F X U I E N D I N L F G A
I T L R P K R F E E L I N G S
N H T I A R C N T D G M U S E
U G S E M R E W A R D I N G R
I I P N G I P S G M A T Y G V
G S I I U K T N S F T E S V I
R N R A N N I A D I F D H O C
O I I E L N O N T A O R L I E
W E T L E C N E D I F N O C S
O S U K A L S Y S N O P H E A
L R A I S E L B A R E N L U V
L W L N H G H T N E S S M W
A I T H O T H E E R A H S R S
```

Allow	Heartfelt	Speak
Awakening	Insight	Spiritual
Confidence	Kindness	Truly
Empathy	Limitations	Unique
Expand	Love	Unleash
Expression	Open	Unlimited
Feelings	Perceptions	Voice
Gifts	Rewarding	Vulnerable
Grow	Service	
Healing	Share	

Creating a New Life

On the deepest level of consciousness, radical spiritual transformation is taking place within each of us. Pay attention. Participate!

The last few years have given us the opportunity to take a good look and see what or who we need to let go of. It is enough to just identify them, write them down and keep track of them. Add and delete like a To Do list. Work as Spirit leads.

Release all that mental busy-ness by fixing attention on a beautiful image. Go outside and look at the trees, the clouds, the plants and the flowers. Connect with nature. Feel grateful for this beautiful Planet. Let mental struggle go. Find a sense of renewal.

Releasing the old and creating the new is an important spiritual process. As we move into our new lives, the old duality must pass away. Where are those old patterns holding us back? Inhibiting change? Let go of that which no longer serves. Free up space for the new.

Mantra:

— —— ——————— ———
——— —— — ——— —————
——— ———

```
T K C A R T C I A E L M M R Y
E R U T A N O E E T U L E L T
A S A E A S N F T A F A N S I
T I E N N G S L E P I C T P L
T G T E S H C O L I T I A I A
E R Y L R F I W E C U D L R U
N A F G E T O E D I A A E I D
T T I G N T U R O T E R L T S
I E T U E E S S M R B D S S O
O F N R W G N E I A C S E A N
N U E T A N E B P P T N S U I
L L D S L A S D T E Y I H A E
E T I R W H S E S S E C O R P
I M A G E C L O U D S D N N E
S T N A L P W B R E L E A S E
```

Attention
Beautiful
Busyness
Change
Clouds
Consciousness
Deepest
Delete
Duality
Flowers

Grateful
Identify
Image
Mental
Nature
Participate
Pass
Plants
Processes
Radical

Release
Renewal
Spirit
Struggle
Track
Transformation
Trees
Write

Breakdown

Take a look at what is breaking down in your life. Is something crimping your style? Think about how to get a handle on it. Remember that virtually every major breakthrough is preceded by a breakdown.

Any current or impending breakdown occurring in your life needs nurturing and creative attention. Any kind of challenge that comes your way, or is presently in your face, is really a gift in disguise.

No shame. No blame. Stay positive no matter what seems to jump up to interfere with your joy. Use all the tools you have acquired along the way. You are amazing! You are effective and marvelous! This Oracle validates you and all your hard work.

Talk with someone of like mind who can support you being you. Stay connected at the heart level. These transformations are here to teach us. Breakdowns and breakthroughs expand our thinking, feeling and subtle energy levels.

Mantra:

___ ____ __
_____ _____ _
__ _____ _____ _
_____ _____
_____ __ _____
_____

```
L E V E L I T S O K D A T T T Y
T T O B L R E A K D O N R R W N
B E E P C D E R I U Q C A O A U
S A M A Z I N G N I D N E P M I
E U I A C M S A I C S V H P X B
J R E N O H A U H F I U K U I E
N G B U N S L O O T T R B S T H
R C O R N U G R C L H S E T S O
M H E T E T M E H R E S I H L F
N A G U C A F W O T I V H I T E
C L H R T F K J A U Y M R S U E
P L P I E O A D G R G T P A S L
M E O N D M I S O Y R P E I M I
R N S G O L I N A W E L D E N N
S G V E A D L T H I N K I N G G
O E E V I T A E R C E P M E N T
```

Acquired
Amazing
Breakdown
Challenge
Connected
Creative
Crimping
Disguise
Effective
Energy

Etheric
Expand
Feeling
Gift
Handle
Heart
Impending
Jump
Level
Major

Marvelous
Nurturing
Subtle
Support
Teach
Thinking
Tools
Transformations
Validates

34   **Freedom**

Feeling impatient with folks? Maybe even with yourself and your spiritual progress? That there is never enough time, money, energy, people, or support? That vision of lack is really a myth.

We have unlimited time spiritually. The new level of consciousness we have just begun brings with it timelessness. No limiting thoughts. Contemplate this. Step into desire to be free from struggle and stress.

How do you relinquish impatience, anxiety, guilt, worry, or whatever it is for you? Tell yourself that everything, all of life, is moving at the perfect pace. Everything that is happening is supposed to happen. You are in the right time and the right place. It is wonderful. Even though there are stresses beyond imagination, free yourself to know that all of it is in harmony with the universe. Know this too shall pass. Always, always, always bring yourself back to the present moment. With this peace, with this awareness, with this understanding we are able to relax more and more into the freedom of being who we truly are. Savor all of life's preciousness!

Mantra:

_____ ___ __ ____
_____ __ __ _____
____ _ __ _____
____ ___ _____ ____
___ _____ __ ___ _
__ __

```
T H E P R T E U A A R E D N O
T I M L E L N I M N I E T S O
H P N A T I M E M X T Y S P I
T S R C V M P R S I I T S W O
Y R I E T A L P M E T N O C K
M I R U C G U I L T R I G H T
P S O E Q I L A N Y M P R E L
E A V X L N O E L G G U R T S
A I A N U A I U G M Y O C F R
C E S A N T X L S S S E R T S
E P D M A I W O E N F E N R E
I N A P T O L U F R E D N O W
O T M S R N H E E D F S R E M
E I D R S U P P O R T O S M O
F W Y H Y N O M R A H O I A M
```

Anxiety	Pass	Stress
Contemplate	Peace	Struggle
Freedom	Perfect	Support
Guilt	Place	Time
Harmony	Preciousness	Universe
Imagination	Present	Unlimited
Impatient	Relax	Wonderful
Money	Relinquish	Worry
Myth	Right	
Pace	Savor	

Balance

Staying balanced?

Things come up in life. Events can lay us low or throw us off balance. We react! Sometimes inappropriately, with anger or defensiveness. Then we wish we could take it back. Keeping equilibrium and not being thrown off balance, no matter what has come up, is a powerful practice.

Take each instance just as it is. Let it be; allow it to be so. Do not fight it. Do not let the mind pick up the old repeated lines. Let those thoughts flow on by without engaging them. When things flow, we know that our core center of balance will be maintained.

Stay on an even keel and flow with the river of life. Not too high, not too low. Staying balanced does not mean standing still, or staying in one place. To maintain equilibrium, we need to move: a little here, a little there, then a little here…think of the tightrope walker. Balance is paramount.

Mantra:

— —— —————— —
———————— —— ————— —
————————— —— —— ————— —

```
E S E N I L A W N I T L A M S
S C T A Y L P I E I H M E N G
R S I B A I P S V L R U A E N
C E E T E T R H E E O I D A K
C G A N C S O T P L W R L E E
R O N C E A P A M T N B A V P
E E R I T V R R I T R I V E O
A V K E Y A I P N I E L R C R
N O Y L M A A S D L V I E N T
G M I O A E T N N T I U T A H
E E U R S W E S V E R Q N L G
R N N I A T N I A M F E I A I
T A O L O C E N T E R E D B T
F P G N I D N A T S M Y D L I
A L L O W F P O W E R F U L E
```

Allow	Keel	React
Anger	Lines	River
Appropriate	Little	Standing
Balance	Maintain	Staying
Centered	Mind	Still
Core	Move	Thrown
Defensiveness	Paramount	Tightrope
Equilibrium	Poise	Walker
Even	Powerful	Wish
Interval	Practice	

36 Clearing

These transformational times are calling for a clearing of past vows, connections and relationships. We are at a stage of human consciousness where we have the potential for everything.

Come clean. Divorce yourself from long-held beliefs and concerns. Look at them in a new light to see if they still work. Stop the mind. Listen to the heart. Listen to the inner voice. Turn up the volume. Quiet the internal chatter. Erase that which you intuitively know has no current relevance.

Practice intervention when you find your mind has taken you down a path. Catch yourself before heading down the rabbit hole! You know very well what I am talking about. The mind plays scenarios that really have nothing to do with anything…what we shoulda, coulda, woulda done. Catch it! Stop it! Clear it now! Erase all of that! It has no meaning. Say it aloud. Our guides and angels are constantly sending us information and messages. Connect with them. Clear your space. Make room. Come back to present time, back to the NOW! Clearing is expansion.

Mantra:

_ _____ _____

_____

_____ __ _

_____ ____

_____ __

_____ __

_____

```
I C L E H C T A C O N N E C T
E R A S E A R F R E P O T S E
L Y E W E N P R A C T I C E T
H U S O I G A S T I C T H C A
L L Y V H E A F E M A A A R R
L E S S O D X S L O Y M T O A
S I G R L A F P S M S R T V P
N T C U E E P O A E H O E I I
E S O L I R I T M N M F R D O
T H P L E R R E P T S N O R T
S U E S A A A N N I Q I C T Y
I B E N B N R T E M U L O V T
L N E B I O R I E X I P U N A
T C I N N A D A N M E N L Y C
S T G O E N S L C G T I D O U
S N E H T A P W O U L D A S S
```

Beliefs	Hole	Present
Catch	Information	Quiet
Chatter	Listen	Rabbit
Clearing	Meaning	Scenarios
Connect	Messages	Shoulda
Coulda	Mind	Stop
Divorce	Moment	Volume
Erase	Path	Vows
Expansion	Potential	Woulda
Heart	Practice	

37 Fired

Some job or responsibility is no longer bringing you satisfaction. It is time to fire yourself!

We get caught up in something we think we have to continue to do to be a responsible person, or to be considered someone reliable. This can sometimes be a good thing. Other times, we get in a rut and forget to consider whether what we are doing is out of obligation, or is really something we value.

Outgrow something. Relinquish that which no longer serves. It doesn't necessarily mean we need to leave our spouse or quit our job, but then again it may. Really, only you know what dead branch needs to be cut away to strengthen your whole tree, and provide room for new growth.

No matter what it is, intuition is telling you now is the time. Take the risk. Take the leap! Do it now.

Mantra:

— ———— — ———— ———— ——
—— ———— —————————
——— ——— —— ————— ————
—— ———— ————— —— ——
——— ———— — ——— —— ——

```
I T S P A C E C O U N T A K E
A G O A O N W O N K E D L O O
K A T M T O Y O L W H O L E I
F E E S I I I F C T T U A T I
O U N A N T S A I D G L E M E
T N O H I A U F M R N Y L I H
E I U U S G A R A E E T B S T
E T T L H I L M D C R D I T E
D N G T C L U I W H T T S A A
I O R T N B V Q V N S I N K E
E C O D A O S T N A O U O E G
O D W G R O W T H I L Q P N A
N D N P B T H P A E L U S E N
I K S I R L S P O U S E E E T
I T G O M C O N S I D E R E D
```

Branch	Leap	Satisfaction
Caught	Mind	Space
Considered	Mistaken	Spouse
Continue	Obligation	Strengthen
Count	Outgrown	Value
Fired	Provide	Whole
Good	Quit	
Growth	Relinquish	
Intuition	Responsible	
Know	Risk	

38

Forgiveness

Forgiveness allows us to tap into the immense beauty and opportunities that lie beneath emotional scars. Unbury and unburden from past actions, events, grievances, perceived insults or disrespect. Free up the energy tied to old feelings and failures. Free the spirit.

Forgiveness comes through turning attention inward. Use the spiritual energy of love to assess relationships.

Many have past traumas that have not been dealt with. We don't know what to do with that feeling of being a victim. Bring these things up. Stop thinking about them. Release them into the ethers where they are transmuted. This frees us.

The act of forgiveness is a spiritual initiative rather than a rational experience. It is not grounded in the emotions or intellect. It is not the rational mind that forgives; it is the heart.

Mantra:

— —— ———— —— —————————
—— ——————————
———————— ———
—————————— ———— —
———— ———— — —— ————
—— ———— —— ————

```
S P I H S N O I T A L E R I A M
T S R U E T O M Y S D E L F T H
B Y E V I T A I T I N I F R E E
F O R N G I L A N O I T A R V A
I I M M E N S E N G M N T E S R
V N E R C V D Y O N S E T S A T
N S L A N O I T O M E D E I E N
V U S C A R S G U E R S N Y F E
T L H T V I R T R N S T T A G D
T T Y I E H E E A O E T I I E R
M S T O I D S T E L F L O D E U
T A U N R T P H L H U E N R N B
I P A S G A E E T R A U M A S N
M D E V I E C R E P O F R W E U
E T B O L T T S I R V E I N N L
O V U N B U R Y G V I C T I M E
```

Actions	Grievance	Perceived
Assess	Grounded	Rational
Attention	Heart	Relationships
Beauty	Immense	Scars
Disrespect	Initiative	Transmuted
Emotional	Insults	Traumas
Ethers	Intellect	Unburden
Failure	Inward	Unbury
Forgiveness	Mind	Victim
Free	Past	

Potential

39

Potential has opened up! We have shifted from galactic consciousness into universal consciousness. There is an inflow of love energy. Stay tuned to the potentials in your life. Potential is there for family, loved ones, friends, our world and our planet. Fear does not have to be part of the experience.

Accept personal responsibility for the events that have unfolded in life. Forgive others. Move into potential completely connected to the Divine Pipeline. Anticipate success. Meaningful relationships will flow to you. Allow your creative expression to reflect your connection with Spirit.

The Love energy brings potential. There will be healing on a massive scale. It is not necessary that we do anything in particular. Continually step more and more into the true authentic self. Be the change you want to see. Live the example. Stay balanced and centered amidst the strong inflow of the potentials. Expand the potential for love and joy. Embrace happiness. Remember all you need is love!

Mantra:

— —— —————————— ——
———— ————————— ———
—— —— ———————

```
R I A D E R E T N E C S E L F
M E R E C R E A T I V E A E H
D L S G A L A C T I C I N N E
Z I A P E X A M P L E I M O A
I E V U O N G M W O L L A I L
S N U I T N Y F U E A F S S I
U E S N N H S S P I L E S S N
C R L S I E E I T P O A I E G
C G W T E V P N B R E R V R T
E Y C O N N E C T I O N E P C
S N T E L T I R E I L N I X E
S A E L O F A P S L C I G E L
N D D P I T N I P A A S T A F
E V I G R O F I M A L C A Y E
Z I B A L A N C E D H N S G R
```

Allow	Expression	Pipeline
Authentic	Fear	Potential
Balanced	Forgive	Reflect
Centered	Galactic	Responsibility
Connection	Happiness	Scale
Creative	Healing	Self
Divine	Inflow	Strong
Energy	Massive	Success
Example	Need	Universal

40   **Joy**

Step into joy!

We can get so caught up in everyday life, thinking and routines that we forget to remember joy. Take a step back. Let some joy in! We all touch it, here and there along the way. Is that enough? Look at what brings joy to our world. Children, grandchildren, friends, work, significant others, creative expression, whatever it is, allow that joy to fill you up. Now is a great time. Take a look around. Open your heart.

Be joyful, confident and grateful that you are alive. All really is well. Enjoy that feeling. Bring it into your heart, feel it fully. Feel the joy of life flowing through every cell, every moment!

Mantra:

— ———— ———— ——— ———
—— ————— ——— — ——
————— ———— ————— ———

```
K G C L U F Y O J I L T Y S T
E R N R L P I T N T U H L W O
Y R O I E I R N T H F I L O E
A O T W E A F A J N E N U R O
D U H Y E B T C O L T K F L O
Y T E H Y L F I B I A I E D C
R I R I O O S F V F R N N O C
E N S O P S J I G E G G N H F
V E K W E S D N E I R F I A T
E S H R N T O G E I I L M L H
A M P R N O I I G D D I H I G
T X H E E U R S E R L E R V I
E I G H S C T N E Y N O W E R
F E E L S H T N G N I W O L F
```

Alive	Fill	Others
Being	Flowing	Right
Children	Friends	Routines
Confident	Fully	Significant
Creative	Grateful	Thinking
Enjoy	Heart	Touch
Everyday	Joyful	Work
Expression	Life	World
Family	Look	
Feel	Openness	

Cristina's Commentary - Mantra

It's one thing to read about the amazing life altering benefits of this stuff, but how does it work in the real world? Is it truly doable? Is it actually worth it? Why even bother?

Here's the inside scoop. Mantras can be a total game changer or not work at all. It depends. The key to success is you. What are you willing and able to do?

I am not one to take claims of the extraordinary rewards of any product or practice at face value. I need to try it and experience the results for myself. Over decades of deep diving into personal evolution, I have experimented with mantras and positive affirmations. These powerful techniques work for me. The favorable outcomes are reliable and repeatable. The yoga of mantra has become a valuable tool; it has helped me craft a life I love.

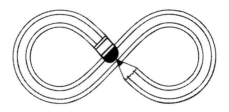

The treadmill, the lap swimming pool and the car have been the most frequent places I have recited countless repetitions of positive affirmation mantras. I say them both aloud and silently to consciously reprogram negative thought patterns. The newly rewired belief circuits are created after a month of consistent enthusiastic effort. Applying desire and discipline to intentionally improve my life through the yoga of mantra, my happiness quotient increases every time!

[happiness]

Silent mantra is a wonderful method to help keep my mind from driving me crazy. When the inner chatter becomes a hubbub of blah blah, I whip out my trusty mind management mantra. **I have the right to a quiet mind.**

Don't take my word for it! Feel free to experiment with it yourself. Practice saying it over and over again inside your head when out for a walk or workout or doing the dishes. It can help bring more serenity, happiness and joy to your inner world. That will then reflect in your outer world. **I have the right to a quiet mind.**

When the mind jumps on the inner hamster wheel of a thought path that no longer serves, start saying the mantra. Over and over and over again. **I have the right to a quiet mind.**

> The more we are able to quiet the mind,
> the easier it is to hear the invisible realms.

> Mantras help.

I have the right to a quiet mind.

Appreciation

First let me say how much I love and appreciate you! Thank you for being you.

Gratitude is the base from which appreciation grows and flourishes. Appreciation carries a vibrational difference from gratitude. Appreciation is more active; it is in personal alignment with who you are.

You can feel the subtle difference, yes? For example, we are grateful for the food we have to eat. We appreciate the colors, the smells, the beauty, the arrangement, and the tastes. Yummy!

Be grateful and then appreciate. This subtle shift involves being more present and thoughtfully aware. Reflect on the reasons to be grateful for someone or something.

Awaken the feelings of loving, self-affirming appreciation. Take every opportunity to let others in your life know how much you appreciate them. Be specific; it truly warms the soul and connects you at the heart level. Remember everyone blossoms under the sunshine of having their value noticed and appreciated.

Mantra:

— —— ————— ————
————————————
——— ————

```
I N T Y U M M Y S H I F T A M
A E T C S F I C D O O F A L S
F K L H E L O S O U L E P G M
F A A E O L L D W S I V P R O
I W T W O U F E P H A I R A S
R A R R A N G E M E N T E T S
M Y S P S R C H R S T C C I O
I T P M R I E E T R C A I T L
N U R I F A T I A F O N A U B
G A L I G N M E N T U F T D E
W E C E N I H S N U S L E E T
O B R L S E H S I R U O L F S
G N I V O L D E C I T O N Y A
I E U L A V E L T B U S F E T
```

Active	Flourishes	Specific
Affirming	Food	Subtle
Alignment	Gratitude	Sunshine
Appreciate	Heart	Taste
Arrangement	Loving	Thoughtfully
Awaken	Noticed	Value
Aware	Reflect	Warms
Beauty	Shift	Yummy
Blossoms	Smells	
Colors	Soul	

Silent Counsel

Asking others for advice? Seeking help from outside yourself? Go to your Higher Self, to intuition, guides and angels. Inquire within. Follow Spirit, your silent counsel, without hesitation. Listen inside for advice and direction.

Entering into this space pulls us into being still. Being still is a powerful response to any situation. Stillness is the favorite strategy of those who have real mastery in life. Just being quiet, but fully alert will usually bring a situation to its own resolution. It is the wisest part of us that knows how to pause once in a while and contemplate. Be like a hawk in a tree watching, waiting, expecting...ready!

Stillness, pausing, quieting to connect with silent counsel is not about denial or passivity. It is about bringing a quality of presence to life. This allows us to breathe easier, to be calmer and more patient. We become a sign post for others as we become still and at peace with ourselves. Whatever is going on, listen within.

Mantra:

— —— —————————————
—————— ——— —————
—————— ——— ———————

```
I A N R S M P A U S E Y W W A
Y D A E R S H P L P G R I A E
T C I S T A E C T E I N T I L
G E M O Y S S N T T R E H T E
T L I L E F I A L A A T I C S
S N N U D X R L E L W G N Y N
E T E T Q T P R O P I E I T U
S N H I S D I E R M S T N I O
I E A O T U E G C E W I S L C
W L W N Q A T S R T M H I A B
N I K N F O P P I N I L R U E
G S I R E N N I U O I N A Q I
Y R E T S A M D A C P N G C N
E C A E P C E B R E A T H E G
```

Alert	Listen	Resolution
Being	Mastery	Silent
Breathe	Patient	Stillness
Calmer	Pause	Strategy
Contemplate	Peace	Wait
Counsel	Poised	Watch
Expecting	Presence	Wisest
Hawk	Quality	Within
Inner	Quiet	
Inquire	Ready	

Challenge

We are all truly going through a lot right now. It is different for each person. The challenge is to finish up old business and breakthrough past and outworn behaviors. Move life forward!

The true challenge is our willingness to face our own inner demons. Do you place limits on yourself? What stops you from what you want? Go into these places; look at the shadow side. Acknowledge your truth. It is a real initiation.

No one has to come up with and do everything alone. Relax into and accept the guidance that is coming through intuition. Listen up! Allow it to be easy. Allow yourself to be guided. Breathe.

Trust your dreams and visions. Release that which tells you that you are unable or can't do what you want. Realize it is Divine Love that brings our dreams and visions into actuality.

Mantra:

__ __ __ _____ __ __

_____ ___ _____ __ _____ ____ _ ____

```
S I T A M L I S T E N I V I D
A M S W A K E N V I S I O N S
I X A L E R N G M Y W D H I R
E A P E M S D E D I U G A T N
D C B H R W O L L A U O O I S
I N R E G D E L W O N K C A Y
G B E H A V I O R S D R F T T
D O A M O N D H S R E E I I A
E T T L G A T E A A V L N O N
M R H N H K N W L O A E I N I
O U E S A I R I M U E A S Y F
N S E E S O Z S T T W S H H A
S T R U F E T C A C C E P T I
W B B A C H A L L E N G E N T
```

Accept	Divine	Past
Acknowledge	Dreams	Realize
Actuality	Easy	Relax
Allow	Finish	Release
Behaviors	Forward	Shadow
Breakthrough	Guided	Trust
Breathe	Initiation	Visions
Business	Listen	Willingness
Challenge	Love	
Demons	Move	

Setback

For every so-called setback, there exists a new possibility. One step back can mean two steps ahead.

A setback is simply a matter of interpretation. You cannot be set back unless you are moving ahead. These challenges give the opportunity to put spiritual tools into practice. Choose how to react or respond. Decide to forgive with understanding and compassion. Would you rather stir up drama? It is all about who we choose to be. Right here. Right now.

To consider setback as a negative is to risk real failure and a long recovery. A positive, yet realistic, understanding leads to success. These challenges create conditions for necessary purifying, cleansing, and rebalancing. They plant new seeds of opportunity.

Out of setback comes learning and new growth. It is there to let us know there is another, better way.

Mantra:

__ ____ ___
_____ __ ____
____ ____ ____ ____
_____ ___
_____ __
____

```
I M H E E T F O R G I V E T H
E T C A E R S C R I S K V H A
L L E N T S E E A G L R I E S
I N L I E R C F H R E T T E B
E W I C U O E M E B A T A D H
E Y C L V A O D A O R A G I E
S U I E M V W L D I N N E C D
S A R A I E A A O P I G N E E
F Y R N N N L U O Y N E O D C
K D G S C I N T F G G R F O H
R Y T I L I B I S S O P O P O
P O N N R T R R E S P O N D O
U G N G I U T I I E X I S T S
T N A L P E S P O S I T I V E
T O G T O O L S E E D S R O W
```

Ahead	Hatred	Recovery
Anger	Learning	Respond
Better	Moving	Risk
Choose	Negative	Road
Cleansing	Plant	Seeds
Decide	Positive	Spiritual
Drama	Possibility	Success
Exists	Purifying	Tools
Failure	React	
Forgive	Rebalancing	

45   Inherent Wisdom

Inherent wisdom is that level of knowledge that comes from the universal collective unconscious and your own spirit within that collective. It is not learned; it is innate, known at the deepest level.

Tap into this level within. Find its source at your heart center. Express it out to the world. Use it in your meditations or prayers.

Inherent wisdom brings with it a calm and reflective sense of self, a knowingness of the truth in any situation. Open your eyes, ears and heart. You will intuit the truth.

Part of accessing this inherent wisdom is acknowledging that we have the ability to see to the bottom of things. Listen and sound out the truth. No need to be blown about by what others say. Sink an anchor into your own heart; bring forth your inherent wisdom.

Mantra:

—   —————— —— ————————
————— —— ————— ——
——————— ————

```
H T U R T T S O U R C E I A L
U S O U N D N L A W I T H I N
M N I O O G W E M N Y I C N H
E L D N R R N E M I C O N T W
I E A E K I M I N O L H T S R
R Y D C R O G H S L M I O E U
O E M T D S E I E S U O F R N
I S T S A R T C N T E L G L I
U N I N E B T A N A E C E T V
I W N N E I I N C L V C R E
D E T A V C M L T D E E N A R
S R A E T T H I I L I E R E S
N W O L B E V O U T P N G H A
K N O W L E D G E O Y H G L L
I F E B O T T O M N E T S I L
```

Ability
Accessing
Anchor
Blown
Bottom
Calm
Center
Collective
Ears
Eyes
Heart

Inherent
Innate
Intuit
Knowledge
Level
Listen
Moment
Open
Original
Reflective
Sink

Sound
Source
Truth
Understanding
Universal
Wisdom
Within

46   Purpose

Life is better when we have a purpose. It can be a simple, humble goal of being of service to others, or a large intention to help support the changes happening on this planet. The important part of our purpose is to feel it has value.

Take a look at identifying your purpose. Appreciate the value you bring to this Earth. Embody your purpose. This will provide inspiration and direction.

Feel without purpose? Meditate on what it is you do. How do you contribute to All That Is? What makes you happy? It can be as personal as becoming the more true you, which is an excellent purpose. Not static, purposes are dynamic. They change as we find ourselves and the world around us changing.

Mantra:

— — — — — — — — — — — — — — —
— — — — — — — — — — — — — —
— — — —

```
T N E L L E C X E Y D G I A E
L M T C S O C M L Y P N O L T
A E R I M E O I N O E P B A P
R N U G N R G A T S O M A A L
G O E N E S M N O A U K P H C
E I L I S I P P A H T P A O I
T T S Y C E R I W H R S N N M
A N I F T U R O R E C T O S P
T E M I P I R V C A R I U N O
I T P T G L T I I I T P H Y R
D N L N D E A L B C P I D P T
E I E E U T E U E O E O O R A
M P O D E E R R S B E O N N
F M Y I F E I T L M L I F E T
E U L A V D I T E N A L P F E
```

Appreciate	Humble	Planet
Changes	Identifying	Purpose
Contribute	Important	Service
Direction	Inspiration	Simple
Dynamic	Intention	Static
Embody	Large	Support
Excellent	Life	True
Feel	Look	Value
Goal	Meditate	World
Happy	More	

47   **Willingness**

What is holding you back? Keeping you from feeling free? Is there something still hanging you up? Be willing to let it go! Move into the next step.

We all come into the world fully prepared to participate in community. We are destined to create meaningful interactions. Check out what your expectations of others are. We can truly only be responsible for our own actions. Be willing to expand and improve perceptual skills. Perceive, intuit and read the intentions, energies and unspoken words of others.

Non-verbal communications are the language of the universe. They are shared by all living things. Willingness offers insight into ways to create community. Spiritual growth will be served by some quiet reflection on the nature of life. All will be revealed. Be willing!

Mantra:

__   __   _____   __

_____   ___   _____

__   _____   _____

```
I Q A M W I L A U T I R I P S
T L U W L D E V R E S I E A P
H Y H I D N X G T O S X I R E
G T T L E M P P R N P O E T T
I I W L S T E E O A V E V I S
S N O I T A C I N U M M O C U
N U R N I G T D A E N D R I N
I M G G N N A S A V R E P P I
N M X P E I T N N I A G M A V
T O N T D G I O A E D M I T E
U C N Y K N O I T C E L F E R
I I P C G A N T U R E R R C S
T E E F P H S C R E A T E T E
U H U A L S K A E P I L E L S
C L A N G U A G E S K I L L S
```

Actions	Growth	Perceive
Check	Hanging	Quiet
Communications	Improve	Reflection
Community	Insight	Served
Create	Intentions	Skills
Destined	Intuit	Spiritual
Energies	Language	Steps
Expand	Meaningful	Universe
Expectations	Nature	Willing
Free	Participate	

48   **Perception**

Intuition is opening and expanding. We can feel what others are saying or feeling, whether they are speaking the truth or not. It is almost like being psychic, right?

This ability has always been part of the human psyche. It is really coming forward now. Heightened perception is here to discern what is really going on beyond the surface of daily life.

When our perception points out the truth or falsity of situations, or things being said, it does not necessarily mean there is anything for us to do other than observe it. Use perception to stay in sovereignty. Don't get pulled into the dramas of others. Perception is the witness which keeps us clear and protected. If it is heavy drama, surround yourself with white light. Imagine mirrors all around, with the shiny side out so that nothing but truth and positive can enter your space. Stay aware and alert. Honor your perceptions!

Mantra:

__ __ __ __ __ __ __ __ __ __ __ __ __

__ __ __ __ __ __ __ __ __ __

__ __ __ __ __ __ __ __ __

__ __ __ __ __ __ __ __ __

```
F E E L I N G C I H C Y S P I
S A Y I N G R A E L C P S E A
S O V E R E I G N T Y R E T M
L R D P N I A V S I N O N I A
B G O E I O N M T P T T H W
E H E R N T I H A L A E I W A
Y I G C R E G T H R P C W T R
O O F E M I T O I O D T E D E
N E L P L Y M H S U N E E R E
D A V T S E T I G R T D C V C
T O N I R T T I E I N N R Y A
R S C O L I N C S A E E I N F
U I N N V A S I P L S H O I R
T O U E S I P X O B A E R H U
H C E P D T E I O P O F N S S
```

Alert	Heightened	Psychic
Alive	Honor	Saying
Aware	Intuition	Shiny
Beyond	Light	Sovereignty
Clear	Mirrors	Space
Discern	Observe	Surface
Drama	Perception	Truth
Expanded	Points	White
Falsity	Positive	Witness
Feeling	Protected	

Now

How often do we think about what happened yesterday? How about last month or even five, ten, or twenty years ago? We worry about what's going to happen tomorrow, or next year, or seven years from now.

We cheat ourselves of experiencing life to the fullest by living in the past or the future in our minds. We miss out on being in the present moment. We don't feel, taste or smell what is happening right in front of us.

If you find yourself driving along and realize you are off on some fantasy mind trip that has nothing to do with the present reality, call yourself back. Focus. Check out what is going on. Stay present with the traffic. Use the mantra to bring you back to right here, right now.

Bring your awareness into this moment. True heart connection can only happen in the present. Be here now.

Mantra:

__ __ __ __ __ __ __ __ __ __ __ __ __ __ __ __

__ __ __ __ __ __ __ __ __ __ __ __ __

```
E F E E L Y T I N A Y T M R
F X U A A T T N M E O A I L
L Y P D W W S O E M V G T P
R E O E E A M E O S H E N S
H T S N R E R R L T E O S E
E E T C N I R E Y L I R M R
E Y A T H O E S N T U A P U
N T T R W E A N C E N F M T
E I S P T T C E C T S N I U
T R I A N H N K R I P S N F
E R E A T N H A E R N A D E
T H F H O S U C O F A G S N
C D N C Y E S T E R D A Y T
O W T R A F F I C Y E A R S
```

Awareness	Heart	Taste
Cheat	Here	Today
Check	Mantra	Tomorrow
Connection	Mind	Traffic
Experiencing	Moment	Trip
Fantasy	Past	Twenty
Feel	Present	Years
Focus	Right	Yesterday
Fullest	Seven	
Future	Stay	

Trust

An acceleration of spiritual growth is occurring which will change our definition of love. Now there is sufficient courage to radically trust in new ways.

Know in your heart that love is a state of being. In that state of being, maintain trust. No matter your fears or insecurities, trust yourself. You are worthy. You really, really are! No matter your fears or insecurities, trust yourself. Bring yourself to a greater clarity of love.

We are all yearning for love. It is time to deepen that capacity within ourselves. That includes loving yourself and trusting yourself every step of the way. Know that you are guided by Spirit, your angels and your guides. Aim for sealing into your being the highest good in every situation. Trust the process. Trust the expression of your True Self. You are totally loveable and loved by God, your angels and many more. Repeat *love and trust*. Make it your mantra. Know you will be guided when the time is right.

Mantra:

_ _____ __ _____
_____ _____ _ __
_____

```
S E A L I N G I G S L E G N A
S G H C H T O N O O S S E T O
C R E T S M I I R W U N U S E
L O A U Y N A C T F O S T M M
A W R E R L A N F I E R B Y E
R T T A F P L I T I N R T X S
I H E L A E C A T R A I P H L
T Y O C N I R I C C A R F A Y
Y V I L E E R C I I E F U E S
E T N N L U E N O S D T K S D
Y N T E C B G S S U I A E O E
W I C E P N E I N R R C R G T
I C S A M E O I I U O A L O A
A N V E D N E P N R R I G H T
I S P A C E S D P G U I D E S
```

Acceleration	Fears	Sealing
Angels	Growth	Space
Being	Guides	Spiritual
Capacity	Heart	State
Clarity	Insecurities	Sufficient
Courage	Love	Trust
Deepen	Mantra	Unseen
Definition	Process	Worthy
Embracing	Radically	Yearning
Expression	Right	

Your Brain on Word Search

Some of the most advanced scientists in the world may know something about you that you don't. Do you realize you are sporting the most complex structure in the universe on top of your shoulders?

The human brain is an exquisite organ. It remains one of the great mysteries yet to be solved. Our brains can make quantum leaps in consciousness, solve complex problems and envision never before seen creations in less than the blink of an eye. Simultaneously!

These three or so pounds of biological software are coalesced in a gel-like, electrically conductive substance within the hermetically sealed skull. Our brains are made up of hundreds of billions of cells with some quadrillion connections between them. These cells fire trillions of electro-chemical signals every second of our lives. That's a lot of zeros!!

That's also a lot of brain to maintain, train and entertain. Psychologists and cognitive scientists have found that solving puzzles engages our ability to compare new information hidden in a puzzle with what is already downloaded in our memory. As a result of our amazing neuroplasticity, neurons make new connections inside our brains, blending imaginative association and memory.

We alchemize that data to pioneer new perspectives, conclusions and ideas. Our freshly uploaded new vision reveals the pattern, or twist that a puzzle conceals. It is a kind of puzzle vision super power. Is it clairvoyance? Expanded intuition? Regardless of the label, the sense is that of absolute knowingness. We experience the perfect harmony of the universe; the solution comes, like magic.

Our 'aha' moment of success is rewarded with a super shot of biochemical brain bliss. Dopamine, the neurotransmitter that helps control the brain's reward and pleasure centers, is released into the brain and gives us that 'I did it!' boost when we accomplish what we set out to do. This great delight makes us want to come back for more pleasure through positive puzzling.

To stay healthy our entire lifetime, we need to exercise the concentration, pattern recognition, and visual perception aspects of our active brains. Word search puzzles are self-directed cognitive training cleverly disguised as fun. By adding the positive affirmations of the mantras into the mix, we are harnessing the power of our brain's inherent suppleness to help reprogram our thinking. Neuroplasticity in action!

Whether it's a devastating trauma, an outdated belief system, or insecurity from school years, our brains can heal. It takes determination, patience and slowing down the mind to perceive and distinguish old patterns. Take positive action. Create a miraculous shift. Once we become conscious operators of our brains, anything is possible.

Going Within

Spend some time focused on the inner reality. So much of our energy is outward bound! Refill your battery.

Create a different mindset. Turn attention inward. Close your eyes and listen to the sound of silence. Notice your inner senses. Explore the inner sight of light, the inner sound of celestial harmony. Experience the inner feelings of spaciousness, and the inner connection to stillness. These subtle senses deserve our attention. Exercise them!

Touch that stillness, that space between thoughts, that space between words. Strengthen the inner senses. This inner awareness will truly help. The outer world can seem to be in chaos. If you do not like what is going on, accept that. On an inner level, know that All is Well. Go within. Sustain yourself with the love of Divine Source.

Mantra:

__ __ _____ _____ __
_____ __ _____ _____ __ _____
_____

```
I S A L G M N G E N E O I N G
W S I O A I T L W C E S H I N
T E I O A I T I I R N T O A I
S N Y T S B T T E O B M S L Y
G S S T U H O S I V A I B I C
S U E S I N R T E A T T T I L
S O U N D L N O N L T U P S I
N I A G L E A W A R E N E S S
I C M H T L O E E Y R C C O H
N A I T C U I N R N Y N C U A
W P A E T B E T W E E N A R R
A S R W E V R E S E D R S C M
R E A R E F I L L N S E G E O
D R T H G I L S E N S E S Y N
D S S I L E N C E R E N N I Y
```

Accept	Going	Senses
Attention	Harmony	Silence
Awareness	Inner	Sound
Battery	Inward	Source
Between	Light	Spaciousness
Celestial	Listen	Stillness
Chaos	Notice	Subtle
Close	Outward	Sustain
Deserve	Reality	Within
Energy	Refill	

52   **Trueness**

The true path is being revealed one step at a time. Feel it in your heart as intuition guides you. Allow more of who you really are to express itself in the world. Let your trueness be revealed. Sometimes we have to be vulnerable to grow.

Let go of the illusion of protecting yourself through superficiality, untruthfulness, and little white lies. Drop the affectations and quit pretending to feel one way while feeling another. It all needs to go away to manifest the new reality.

Each day become more and more into being yourself. Express your true thoughts, your true perspective on reality, and your true heart's knowingness, with authenticity. Express emotions such as anger, annoyance, and irritation by not making someone else wrong, but by saying this is how *I* feel. It's time to be real, folks!

Engage, expand, create and express Trueness with love for self, family, friends, acquaintances, the planet and all the beings thereon. It is who we really are.

Mantra:

— —— ———— ———

——————— —— ———— ————

—— ——————

```
I A T S T E N A L P G I A M O
S A N R D P E G A G N E E N A
S Y F G A N N D Y T I L A E R
E A T F E E E L U P D S C L O
N W L I E R H I R I N S R N E
E A I T C C T O R N E E E O L
U N T G S I T M Y F T R A I B
R N T O E T A R E E P T T A
T O L N C W F N T S R X E A R
U Y E T O E E I E I P E V T E
S A I R E X H I N H O L O I N
F N G T P W L O E A T N L R L
G C F A M I L Y X P M U S R U
R E N R E V E A L E D E A I V
S D P A T H N O I S U L L I S
```

Affectations	Grow	Planet
Anger	Heart	Pretending
Annoyance	Illusion	Protecting
Authenticity	Intuition	Reality
Create	Irritation	Revealed
Engage	Lies	Trueness
Expand	Little	Vulnerable
Express	Love	White
Family	Manifest	
Friends	Path	

53   Choice

All of our choices are either consciously or unconsciously made. They are based on either love or fear. Take a good look at the way you are making your choices. Start changing it up so that your choices are more conscious, more filled with love for whatever is happening. Take the high road at every instance rather than just every now and again.

We all choose things like when to get up, when to go to bed, when to do this or where to do that. We also choose how we react to things that happen in our lives, making thousands of choices every day, either consciously or unconsciously. How we choose to react to things impacts the quality of our lives.

Habit and reactivity lead us to fear based choices. For a happier life, it is a good practice to make conscious choices based on love and kindness. Let go of fear. Choose consciously. Choose love.

Mantra:

— —————— —— ———— ———
———— —— ———— ———
———————— ——————
—————— ——— ——————
——— ——— ————

```
I C R H A P P I E R S F U L L
B A S E D S R D R H D D N I M
O O T R A T A E O C N S E V T
R O A D O C C N M O A Q T E A
K E R E K A T O E N S U T S H
F E T G I P I I P S U A A T T
H E O F N M C T V C O L L I O
V C E A D I E I N I H I D B K
I N N D N N G D E O T T S A C
H A P P E N I N G U S Y T H O
W T A R S G D O A S K L O F M
Y S S E S L O C F H G I H A N
D N O T H E S O O H C E R S A
L I L T H E T I D E V O L M E
```

Release

Release the tensions from all the hard things we have to do in life. Take a deep breath and then let it out, let it ALL go, blessing it all. Take a deep breath of love in and let it flow throughout your being. Let it all out, blessing it. Do that a few more times.

Release is not about giving up or not doing anything; that is a trap. Don't just let go and expect something or someone else to take care of it all. It is our responsibility to pay attention to the forces at play and guide ourselves within the current of the river of our present situation. The energies will support us in going with the flow. Don't resist what is. Enjoy. Allow detachment to be a real part of spiritual practice. This is all a part of life.

Mantra:

── ── ── ── ── ── ── ── ── ── ──
── ── ── ── ── ── ── ── ── ── ──
── ── ── ── ── ── ── ── ── ── ── ──
── ── ── ──

```
A  W  E  S  I  Y  E  X  P  E  C  T  R  T  E
L  O  Y  F  A  T  X  E  A  G  E  N  R  D  S
D  L  A  A  I  I  S  R  C  D  N  O  E  P  E
E  F  L  T  L  L  E  I  I  I  P  I  I  A  R
T  S  P  T  H  I  E  U  T  P  T  R  V  P  A
A  G  R  E  T  B  G  I  U  U  I  C  A  I  C
C  N  E  N  A  I  F  S  A  T  A  R  A  L  G
H  I  S  T  E  S  O  L  U  E  T  T  W  R  D
M  S  E  I  R  N  L  A  Y  N  N  T  I  R  P
E  S  N  O  B  O  L  O  O  S  E  W  A  O  A
N  E  T  N  W  P  R  D  J  I  R  H  E  P  N
T  L  M  Y  H  S  I  G  N  O  R  I  V  E  R
H  B  R  E  L  E  A  S  E  N  U  E  O  E  S
T  G  O  F  O  R  C  E  S  S  C  O  L  D  D
```

Allow	Flow	Release
Attention	Forces	Responsibility
Blessing	Giving	River
Breath	Guide	Situation
Care	Hard	Spiritual
Current	Life	Support
Deep	Love	Tensions
Detachment	Play	Trap
Enjoy	Practice	
Expect	Present	

Expansion

On this journey into our expanded new lives, take notice of the acceleration of time and the arrangement of all events. Practice sensing the movement of those subtle energies of life within our own energy body and within other living systems.

There are many facets to the integration of expansion into spiritual practices. Contemplate and meditate upon the nature of All That Is. Integrate realizations into daily life. This is a time of expansion. Energies have changed.

We have shifted things. We have created new realities and allowed for more and more Light to enter the planet. We are Lighthouses for those who are awakening. Expand love! Expand consciousness. Let your light shine brightly!

Mantra:

— —— ——————— ——
——————————— ———
————————— —— ————
——— —— —————

```
S S U B T L E I M A M E X T P
A E W N D I N E N E R G Y E G
M I C I Y C D O E C I T O N L
N T J I T I S C S O I O A A I
U I S O T H N P A N E C S L G
S L A A U C I W S T C N D P H
R A T A R R A N G E M E N T T
E E X P I K N R L M V R A E H
S R T T E S I E P P N I L G O
M Y U N L O R V Y L E A L G U
N A I R E A L I Z A T I O N S
L N O I T A R G E T N I W I E
G B R I G H T L Y E D M E S N
E V O L Y L S H I F T E D N I
I N D A I L Y G N A T U R E H
H T F A C E T S M E T S Y S S
```

Acceleration	Integration	Realities
Allowed	Journey	Realizations
Arrangement	Lighthouse	Sensing
Awakening	Lives	Shifted
Brightly	Love	Shine
Contemplate	Meditate	Spiritual
Daily	Nature	Subtle
Energy	Notice	Systems
Enter	Planet	Within
Facets	Practices	

Faith

The concept of faith, whatever that means to you, is our bulwark and foundation. Know it. Integrate it. Trust it.

Faith can change, strengthen, lose its grip, or be created anew. We are all moving into a new reality. One thing we need through these changes is some faith.

Faith is one of those words that can conjure up old time religion, ancient mysteries or mysticism. It can also conjure up old programming and limitation, including exclusive belief systems.

Experience faith. Expand the consciousness of faith. Exercise faith: faith in the process, faith in yourself, and faith that all really is well. All the rest is just part of the illusion. The old moves on; the new arises from the ashes.

Trust yourself. Have faith in yourself. Believe in the positive nature of the many changes that are happening on this planet.

Mantra:

— ————— ———————— ———
———— ————— —— ——————

```
T N E I C N A P L A N E T T I
T E X E R C I S E S I R A R N
R U P S S U S T A I N S T U O
F L E S R U O Y H T I A F S I
B E R L M Y S T I C I S M T T
N O I T A D N U O F N I E V A
E N E A N S E I R E T S Y M T
C O N S C I O U S N E S S D I
O I C G N I M M A R G O R P M
N S E R H B U L W A R K A V I
J U N A E F P E R V A D E S L
U L I S A I T E V I T I S O P
R L V P N O I G I L E R H I N
E I I M P R O C E S S E H S A
Y S D N A P X E W O N K E L F
```

Ancient	Faith	Planet
Arises	Foundation	Positive
Ashes	Grasp	Process
Bulwark	Illusion	Programming
Conjure	Integrate	Religion
Consciousness	Know	Sustains
Divine	Limitation	Trust
Exercise	Mysteries	Yourself
Expand	Mysticism	
Experience	Pervades	

Happiness

There are myriad changes going on, daily challenging our emotional, physical and spiritual experiences and processes. We are facing the opportunities to stay balanced and centered in life.

Happiness, that contented, satisfied, comfortable place within, is a touchstone at this time. Happiness is not dependent on outside events or circumstances, or what happened 10, 20, 30 or more years ago.

Being miserable or a victim is a state of mind which keeps us from being happy. Being happy in the most miserable of situations is a state of the heart. Only you can make you happy. Find that place within yourself. Touch it. Be it. Smile. Go ahead. Smile right now!

Mantra:

— —— ————— ———— ————

——— — ——— ——————— ——

```
I E B E A M T T O U C H H S A
P T A M P N D E P E N D E N T
Y A L O E C A L P R O C E S S
C T A T R A E H O O N M E E E
F S N I M I S E R A B L E X V
A O C O M F O R T A B L E P E
C U E N W H A S U S M I L E N
I T D A T M M G N I E B A R T
N S M L Y U N O I T A U T I S
G I Y I C C S A T I S F I E D
A D R R L A U T I R I P S N A
N E I G N I G N E L L A H C I
H C A A L A C I S Y H P N E L
D L D E I C E N T E R E D T Y
```

Balanced	Emotional	Physical
Being	Events	Place
Centered	Experience	Process
Challenging	Facing	Satisfied
Circumstances	Heart	Situation
Comfortable	Miserable	Smile
Content	Myriad	Spiritual
Daily	Opportunities	State
Dependent	Outside	Touch

Gratitude

Gratitude brings amazing changes within mind, body and spirit. Gratitude is a sensation that seems to clear the mind, to bring us back to the present moment. Take a deep breath, right now, while you are reading this. Go ahead. Now, let it out. Take another deep breath and slowly let it out.

Envision the setting of a starry night. Look up into the sky. See all the stars, the planets, see the full moon with its radiance shining down on our planet. Feel connected with the cosmos. Bring in gratitude for those stars, that sky, the earth, the air we breathe, the wind that blows, and the rain that falls. Feel gratitude for your beating heart and for all life forms on this planet. Acknowledge the love you feel. Know that All is Well.

The principle of gratitude is one of the basic tenants of the new world. The daily practice of gratitude can be cultivated as a spiritual experience. Allow yourself to be grateful for what is!

Mantra:

— —— —— —————————— ———
——— ———— ——

```
I A M I D N I W N O O M R N
S E G D E L W O N K C A G E
O H R T A E B A Y D D T C I
M T I U E R L R M I A I D N
S N E N E R P A A T I O F
O I O A I A A N I C Z I L D
C G T C T N C N A C T I E Y
H H S S L E G R T A N E N R
T T P A L E P L S S P I T G
R M I N D H A N A H E A R T
A T R E X P E R I E N C E P
E N I A R S B E A T I N G I
D E T A V I T L U C Y D O B
S T N E S E R P S L O W L Y
```

Acknowledge	Earth	Rain
Amazing	Experience	Sensation
Beating	Heart	Shining
Body	Mind	Slowly
Breath	Moon	Spirit
Clear	Night	Starry
Cosmos	Practice	Tenants
Cultivated	Present	Wind
Daily	Principle	
Deep	Radiance	

Wholeness

Along the path of life, sometimes we feel so incomplete, so unfinished. We pray and we meditate. We sometimes look outside ourselves to fill that incompleteness. We try and fill up that longing, that unarticulated need with people, places and things. Does it work?

Begin to acknowledge that really All is Well. Everything is happening just the way it is supposed to. It is the mind that keeps us pointed in the direction of concern, worry, and fear. As we begin more and more to listen to that small voice inside, we know, beyond the shadow of a doubt that we are indeed whole and complete.

Feel it. Breathe it in. Know it! Wholeness is absolutely a step farther along in the spiritual journey.

Mantra:

— —— ————
— —— ————————
— —— ——— ———— ———
———— ——

```
U I A L M W W P F H P N O L
E N L I O A L E M L R A S C
D I A N O A A R O E E M T P
F I K R C R E N C H T L E H
W S V E T A G N P T E E P T
H E P I L I O T R A L L I A
O M O I N C C B A E P I E V
L N T G R E E U Y R M S C O
E Y W F I I L O L B O T A I
I T E N L T D D A C E P C
H E N R A A L U L E T N S E
L E A M E D I T A T E E T H
R E S W O D A H S L A N D T
H M I N D I Y E N R U O J S
```

Breathe	Journey	Reality
Complete	Know	Shadow
Concern	Listen	Small
Divine	Longing	Space
Doubt	Meditate	Spiritual
Fear	Mind	Step
Feel	Need	Unarticulated
Fill	Path	Voice
Heart	Place	Whole
Inner	Pray	

60 Connecting at the Heart Level

Now is the time to connect with other human beings. In spirit. Online. Energetically. Face to face.

Practice connectedness at the heart level. Flow your love energy out through your heart chakra as you walk your path. Escape the mind; be present in the here and now. Have an open, friendly attitude as you go along your way. Smile!

Look at people, trees, rocks, dirt, animals. All of it! Get out of the head, get into your heart, and look out there in the world. It's about connection, about sending and receiving love. Connect with and trust intuition. Tap into and connect with your higher self, guides and angels. Feel when things or people are not right for you. Be clear. It is wonderful to connect at the heart level with others. We are, indeed, all One!

Mantra:

— —— ——————————— ——
——— —————— —————— ————
——— —————— ——————

H	R	S	M	I	L	E	F	Y	G	R	E	N	E
T	E	N	I	L	N	O	I	L	T	R	E	E	S
A	H	A	N	I	M	A	L	S	O	A	M	C	E
P	G	O	N	C	L	E	A	R	N	W	E	C	D
T	I	I	N	G	N	I	D	N	E	S	I	G	I
C	H	A	F	T	P	R	E	S	E	N	T	N	U
T	O	A	H	E	T	I	R	I	P	S	H	E	G
A	C	N	T	W	O	N	D	E	R	F	U	L	T
E	R	T	N	T	L	S	K	C	O	R	A	R	R
B	R	E	C	E	I	V	I	N	G	N	A	E	U
N	E	L	V	E	C	T	L	W	G	E	I	T	S
A	H	I	O	A	L	T	U	E	H	L	L	I	T
M	V	I	N	V	N	Y	L	D	N	E	I	R	F
U	G	T	H	G	E	S	I	N	E	T	R	I	D
H	N	E	P	O	S	A	R	K	A	H	C	G	S

Angels
Animals
Attitude
Beings
Chakra
Clear
Connect
Dirt
Energy
Face

Flowing
Friendly
Guides
Heart
Higher
Human
Love
Online
Open
Path

Present
Receiving
Rocks
Sending
Smile
Spirit
Trees
Trust
Wonderful

Woo Hoo!
You Did It!
Congratulations!

Great Work!

End Game

We've been on quite a journey together, haven't we?!? Fondly remembering a prayer answered or an imaginary friend, we embrace our many blessings with gratitude. We engage the power of presence and our personal process with fearlessness. Notice your puzzle vision super power improving?

We risk diving in to play, healing, and joy. We let our imaginations run wild. Are you feeling the love? Do your inner and outer worlds feel nourished? Is the glass half full?

Carrying the healing spirit of compassion, we have done some letting go. We have checked our cornerstones and experimented with mantras. We have connected with our eyes. What new things do we now see? With our outer vision? With our inner awareness?

We claim the freedom to savor all of life's preciousness. We feel joy flowing through our cells. We experience inner spaciousness and celestial harmony. We know that we have to be vulnerable to grow. We cannot be set back unless we are moving ahead.

Love or fear? The choice is always ours.

We realize that every human being blooms under the sunshine of having their value noticed and appreciated. We start by noticing and appreciating ourselves. We are seeing dollar bills in a whole new way. Our quiet inner voices have become more audible, and more cherished.

We breathe. We balance. We embody our individual purposes, and explore our wide range of possibilities. We know that all is truly well. We are present in the now.

We engage, expand, create and express our trueness with love. We are lighthouses and teachers. It is who we really are.

We consciously operate our brains, and seek our own Oracle within, knowing there is help and guidance available at every moment.

I have the right to a quiet mind.

This Oracle sees you! Celebrates you!
Values you! Believes in you!

YOU ARE A TREASURE.

Let your light shine brightly!

Answers

Sometimes the answer is in the question.

1. Blessings

2. Relaxation

3. The Power of Presence

4. Support

5. Fearlessness

6. Commitment

7. Power

```
I A M C O N T R I B U T E A
P L A M E N T I N G O A W E
G E N E R A T E R R C V F U
L W B V L N E I E P H O N G
R I G I O E E N S O A I C C
E S L S V G E R P S R D R O
F D E I E A T O I G H E M
U O A O I T N G N T E I A M
S M R N A I N D S I E G T I
E X N P A V N D I V I H E T
N G I A L E I F B E E E S E
N H N L E A D A L N C R I N
G V G L E A P I E P O W E R
S C O M P A S S I O N I O N
```

8. Ambition

```
S H A R E S U P P O R T W I W
F I I N T E G R I T Y P I N O
D A N S I N C E R E D U D E R
S T A A L N D I N A C B E X L
M Y A M E M B I T S O L R C D
I O N B A W I T R P M I E I H
I N T I D E G R E I M C N T O
I T Y T E C O M S R I M E E P
I T M I R E N T P A T A R N E
D R E O S S P O E T N S G I N
B I L N I T Y A C I N D Y L L
O V E S F O R A T O L L T H Y
A A C H I E V E E N G O A L S
F R I E N D S T D S L O V E D
I S E M O T I O N C H O O S E
```

9. Synchronicity

```
I A M P T H C R F U T S G
F O T R E U O I O N R G O
O N F O M M I E U O U V O
C E A C E A N F N P S E D
U N M E R N C R D E T M T
S E I S G E I I A N R O O
Y S L S I D D E T I A T G
Y S Y I N N E N I N E I E
S O U L G V N D O G E O T
B R A I N S C S N R Y N H
E N E R G Y E P L A N S E
N O W A C C I D E N T S R
W A T R A N S I T I O N Y
```

10. Play

```
I R E P V I S I O N S C R
E R L R A T C H I L D I E
L E O E I N N E R E F M M
I L V S L A U G H N A A H
G A E S P W I L L J N G A
H X Y U L W I L D O C I P
T S E R A L F B Y Y I N P
E R E E Y G A M E S F A I
N C J O Y O U S L Y U T N
R J O U R N E Y E A L I E
F A N T A S T I C T I O S
D I S R U P T I O N S N S
L I F E O U N L E A S H N
```

11. Inspiration

```
I N I N O R D I N A R Y T E
N D O M I N D P O W E R T O
B E I T N S P S T A T E I R
A E D A I N F E E L D I E A
M W F I N C D W I D E I A M
N G A I N T E N T I O N S O
W A Y R K B R E A T H E Y M
S T O I E I E X P R E S S E
N A C T S I N S P I R E S N
S T R I K E S D P A I R E T
M Y I N V I T E N S L E L S
D I F F I C U L T E Y E S F
A O P E N L P L E A S U R E
O O T H E R S P A C E S N T
G T H E S I N C E R E W A Y
```

12. Stillness

```
S T I L L N E S S D E E P L Y
P R E S E N T R E A L I Z E I
A M T A O U P R I M A R Y C H
I N G C T H E J S T O P O B Y
O F M R Y G R A T I T U D E B
E I N E J O U R N E Y U H L G
B Y B D C L O S E E I N A I N
G S T O U C H F E E L D P E P
T I L E N C O U R A G E P V R
L A N D S M O M E N T R Y E O
H T H A N K F U L W A L K U C
T T I N G L I S T E N I T H E
E M I N D B L E S S D E O W S
N J F O C U S K N O W S U S S
T F O P A T H R N O L I F E W
```

13. Connection

```
D I S C E R N M E N T A I A
W M C O P E N N E S S V O N
N A E L O O K I N G C A T I
N G L T E N E R G Y V I E W
F E O K P L A C E S M L Y D
F O L I I B R O A D P A T H
R E C I V N R I G H T B I N
F E E U M E G E W O R L D S
S I A L S I E C O N N E C T
N C N L E A N C H O O S E N
D A L I I L I A P E O P L E
L O V E S T S W T H I N G S
E L L I N H Y A L E R T M Y
W O R I N T E G R A T E L D
```

14. Courage

```
I F A M I L Y M O N E Y H A V
T E T H S P I R I T U A L E C
O H P A T H F U T U R E U R A
M O R A L P H Y S I C A L U G
E T O E O P P O S I T I O N W
A L K H A R D S H I P E M P W
F E A R D T Y P A C A C C O A
U N I V E R S E C H T O O P R
C S H T A O S T T A A N U U R
N H H D T A L L I N I O R L I
N M A A H Y T R O G U M A A O
T H A O M N D T N E O Y G R R
B E W H S E C H I L D R E N O
R I G H T S C A N D A L I A M
```

15. Cornerstone

```
C O N S C I O U S N E S S I A
M B M E D I S O L I D T A T I
P E R S O N N G U P O N M Y C
O R N E S T A B L I S H E R R
S T C R A S H P R A C T I C E
O N E A N K D M A S O N R Y A
C H S H I F T A N G N I N G L
I T O R F L O H W I S N G M I
Y F H C O R N E R S T O N E T
G D E C I D E R C O R E A T Y
P I A E T U D X E B U I L D T
L O R I L I D E A S C G T A S
A E T F A I T H I M T B H U I
C L V F O U N D A T I O N D M
E P E E R S Y G N E O N W R E
A L I C L E A N S I N G E T Y
```

16. The Shift

```
C R I P L A N E T C H A O S A
H E F P O S I T I O N W O R K
A L M U A C C E P T A N C E S
N E H A L P R E P A R E T I P
G A F T T F S T R I D E R I A
E S I N G T I B I R T H A M T
P E A C E W E L I T H T N P T
B E L I E V E N L H E N S O E
E P E R S P E C T I V E I R R
W R E A L I T Y R I N E T T N
A L W I L L I N G I O G I A S
I N T E G R I T Y T Y N O N B
H A P P Y B R I L L I A N T R
C O N S C I O U S N E S S T E
S H I F T D E C E P T I O N A
O C O M E D I F F I C U L T K
```

166

17. Mother-Deep

```
S I E A S I L E T E R N A L Y
G T E O W I R I V E R T T H T
H E R A N C I E N T F L R O W
O F E E R V O C E A N E I R Y
T H I N A T F L O W G T C H A
T C O M E M H R A I N S K M Y
C R E A T I O N W A Y A L N D
T H N O U R I S H I N G I E P
S R E B Y R C H A N G I N G R
K R E G E N E R A T E S G E O
I G E N E R M O T I O N A T C
E E E R O D I N G N A T U R E
S M M O T H E R S P I R I T S
Y S E L C O N T I N U O U S S
C O O P E R A T I V E D E E P
F E N D L E S S L Y A L L O W
```

18. Imagination

```
W I A A I M A G I N E L L W O
W I M M A N S W E R Y I M I A
G I N N A A C P L A C E T L I
W I L D O Z N R T S T E P L O
P R U N F R I E E E A N D I L
O G D E T G O N O D F M Y N L
S R R I M I E U G T I I R G N
S O E G B E L N N I E B U L P
I W A A N A L Y T I C A L Y O
B T M F M I N D S E V A E E W
I H S A D D R E S S R E R B E
L O P O T E N T I A L T R O R
I P U T F O U N T A I N A S T
T E H E M I S T A K E S W I E
Y N A Y I S I T U A T I O N N
T I F L O W R E V E A L E D S
```

19. Truth

```
I A S M O B E L I E V E P E S
P N A P T O R O P I N I O N P
E E V B E R E L E A S E C E I
R I I E S A V C R E A T E E N
C A B X L O K L L E D V E L S
E O R P F A L I E V O L V E I
P F A A T A L U N R C U T H D
T A T N N D C L T G T T O M D
I A I D L L O T O E O W M A I
O Y O T R U T H S W R T R S V
N U N E S O V E R E I G N T I
S E L G R O W I N G N N F E D
T E X P R E S S I N G O G R U
M E D I T A T E N G A G E Y A
E X P R E L A T I V E R E S L
S I T S E L S T A N D I N G F
```

20. Desire

```
I H A L I V I N G V E R A R
R P A S S T R A V E L E S E
E E X P R E S S E D I B P A
L A U G H T E R O N A A O D
A N R E K I N D L E D L N Y
X E N J O Y I N N E R A T D
R E J U V E N A T I O N A E
I M P O R T A N T S I C N R
E N E E D S T C E W H E E A
L I F E P A T H H N O E I L
N J F R E E D O M I G O T L
T I M E F A M I L Y L A Y O
Y L P A S S I O N I F D G W
E F R I E N D S D E S I R E
```

21. Encouragement

```
T G U I D E S M A S S I V E T
A R I A M R S O U R C E L E S
L L A E A E N E R G Y S O I U
N G L N O I T N E T T A V T R
M N R O S E M P O W E R E S T
E O Y O W F Y D O B Y R E V E
A I T U B L O E B R S G O V E
N T I R I P S R E E N H E A L
I A N M E H E L M E G I A P A
N T I B I A E T L A L N A S H
G I V A T A N L D E T S A P X
F D I H S A A T B T S I E H E
U E D E R H A N G E L S O N C
L M E N C O U R A G E M E N T
A L O N E S P O S I T I V E S
```

22. Belief

```
I A M E C M H E T S D A E H L
D F A D I L N A H L O V T I N
V I S I B L E G G W A I Y B E
I L K S U S T A I N A B L E N
G T D T I T R E R F F C U T L
Y E N U G R L U F R E D N O W
U R F O C U S E I T I L I B A
I D E D I C C A N D L I V A N
E S G R A T I T U D E T E G R
U V C T A U C E D I B B R G Y
Y R O T I R R E T V T T S A H
E Z I L A E R E N I F N E G O
C O M P A S S I O N R U C E E
N S O F I N S I D E O O H E A
T S U R T V P E R F E C T E N
```

23. Awareness

```
E I B E L C A R O R E A K T H
R N O Y A U G H P A S I K T N
E G L T I R I P S A T N I V E
E A B I L I T Y B L O S S O M
X P E L G G P H R W S I I E N
L E C A C H A L L E N G E S E
S I V T A T T P N Y N H D E E
M O S O T I H E O N P T A D L
P A I T M N R R N T O O I I A
C C E P E A D C T M W R M U Y
D F I V W N I E N E E E N G A
T O U A R G E P L C R N A N D
M C O N N E C T T L F U T E R
G U E P W L I I K C U T S T H
T S H E E S O V D I L D V S I
N E C H A N G E S N E K A W A
```

24. Letting Go

```
F T R U S T C A S I R S R R
L O V E E U E L A M L I E X
O C O U R S E A I A V S N D
W L O R V H E T O E P A K S
S S E N E V I G R O F F S T
G N O I S G C G N F L E I M
T O W T A C L S H I N L R E
L A U T I R I P S E T Y E N
O W E A R B N O R D S T L T
M D E D I U G A U X B T E A
M I A L C Y W H I S A G A L
N O I S S A P M O C N L S H
S T R U G G L E E S K E E T
Y G O O D B R A N C H E S R
G N I D N A T S R E D N U S
```

170

25. Growth

26. Possibility

171

27. Willpower

```
R C I R S U O I C E R P A E M
E C O O E T M Y M I T T N E D
N T E M C P I O L B E O I E R
N N X N P E E L G E L A N L E
I C P O O A R E L A S I V C T
H O A N I I S E D N L I N T N
C M N N E R T S M P E A W N E
U M D G A T Y N I O D S A A C
O I N T F L S C E O N D S H E
T T L L I C S I O T N I M C N
P A O A A I S S L I N A E O G
N W D A D S O U R C E I T S A
T P R A C T I C E S F R E E G
S P I R I T U A L D R U M E E
P E R S O W I L L P O W E R N
```

28. Compassion

```
I N F R S T O L E R A N T U E
A Q E E R R E L I G I O N N L
E S U P S S E S L Y O N E D P
E N P E O N O W S M O Y M E H
E A A E S A O P S I R M H R T
A N T D H T I I S N S D S S
H A I C H R I S T I A N I T Y
R G E E I M A O U A Y L R A T
O V N T E P W D N I N T U N I
H W T I M P N A M S G L O D R
L H I O R I G E N S N C N I U
O O C A H E M B O D I M E N T
U L Y T N N F T I S L A M G A
E E I T R U N F C O A N D D M
R W L I A H D D U B E T I U O
N E V O L A L L Y S H E L P J
```

29. Cooperation

```
I E S S E N C E V O R P M I A
C M C S O D Y O O D I V I N E
E O P E E U U L R A T I N T C
G G O W T C L T D I T H A M N
J E R P N Y O N I R S N E L E
U M E E S F R O T A A N C D
D O T D M R S O P M T W N T I
G C A T N E A E E D M A T H F
E R T O G E R T N S R O S U N
M E I G I N I I E O A C N O
E V L E L E M W L O R P S T C
N O I T A M R O F S N A R T A
T G C H E O T I R I P S W U F
G R A E G N I R E F F U S A P
O W F R I N W A R D L Y D O B
T H T C E P S E R V A L U E S
```

30. Love

```
E A I D N A T S R E D N U P
R L F T S U R T V M C T Y U
U L B F D I V I N E H C F R
T O L A I O T M V R A A I P
L W E F R R A E N G K R T O
U F L D O U M S C I R T N S
C O M P A S S I O N A T E E
W C P F E E L A N G A A D N
I U E C N E S S E G L L I S
S S P L A N E T A M K O A E
M L L O T S I S E R M I V B
R E W S N A V I M A G I N E
W H E A R T E B E A U T Y D
```

31. Expression

```
E M P A T H Y I A M O U P E S
U N E V O L P E X P A N D T T
Q O F X U I E N D I N L F G A
I T L R P K R F E E L I N G S
N H T I A R C N T D G M U S E
U G S E M R E W A R D I N G R
I I P N G I P S G M A T Y G V
G S I I U K T N S F T E S V I
R N R A N N I A D I F D H O C
O I I E L N O N T A O R L I E
W E T L E C N E D I F N O C S
O S U K A L S Y S N O P H E A
L R A I S E L B A R E N L U V
L W L N H G H T H N E S S M W
A I T H O T H E E R A H S R S
```

32. Creating a New Life

```
T K C A R T C I A E L M M R Y
E R U T A N O E E T U L E L T
A S A E A S N F T A F A N S I
T I E N N G S L E P I C T P L
T G T E S H C O L I T I A I A
E R Y L R F I W E C U D L R U
N A F G E T O E D I A A E I D
T T I G N T U R O T E R L T S
I E T U E E S S M R B D S S O
O F N R W G N E I A C S E A N
N U E T A N E B P P T N S U I
L L D S L A S D T E Y I H A E
E T I R W H S E S S E C O R P
I M A G E C L O U D S D N N E
S T N A L P W B R E L E A S E
```

33. Breakdown

```
L E V E L I T S O K D A T T Y
T T O B L R E A K D O N R R W N
B E E P C D E R I U Q C A O A U
S A M A Z I N G N I D N E P M I
E U I A C M S A I C S V H P X B
J R E N O H A U H F I U K U I E
N G B U N S L O O T T R B S T H
R C O R N U G R C L H S E T S O
M H E T E T M E H R E S I H L F
N A G U C A F W O T I V H I T E
C L H R T F K J A U Y M R S U E
P L P I E O A D G R G T P A S L
M E O N D M I S O Y R P E I M I
R N S G O L I N A W E L D E N N
S G V E A D L T H I N K I N G G
O E E V I T A E R C E P M E N T
```

34. Freedom

```
T H E P R T E U A A R E D N O
T I M L E L N I M N I E T S O
H P N A T I M E M X T Y S P I
T S R C V M P R S I I T S W O
Y R I E T A L P M E T N O C K
M I R U C G U I L T R I G H T
P S O E Q I L A N Y M P R E L
E A V X L N O E L G G U R T S
A I A N U A I U G M Y O C F R
C E S A N T X L S S S E R T S
E P D M A I W O E N F E N R E
I N A P T O L U F R E D N O W
O T M S R N H E E D F S R E M
E I D R S U P P O R T O S M O
F W Y H Y N O M R A H O I A M
```

35. Balance

```
E S E N I L A W N I T L A M S
S C T A Y L P I E I H M E N G
R S I B A I P S V L R U A E N
C E E T E T R H E E O I D A K
C G A N C S O T P L W R L E E
R O N C E A P A M T N B A V P
E E R I T V R R I T R I V E O
A V K E Y A I P N I E L R C R
N O Y L M A A S D L V I E N T
G M I O A E T N N T I U T A H
E E U R S W E S V E R Q N L G
R N N I A T N I A M F E I I I
T A O L O C E N T E R E D B T
F P G N I D N A T S M Y D L I
A L L O W F P O W E R F U L E
```

36. Clearing

```
I C L E H C T A C O N N E C T
E R A S E A R F R E P O T S E
L Y E W E N P R A C T I C E T
H U S O I G A S T I C T H C A
L L Y V H E A F E M A A A R R
L E S S O D X S L O Y M T O A
S I G R L A F P S M S R T V P
N T C U E E P O A E H O E I I
E S O L I R I T M N M F R D O
T H P L E R R E P T S N O R T
S U E S A A A N N I Q I C T Y
I B E N B N R T E M U L O V T
L N E B I O R I E X I P U N A
T C I N N A D A N M E N L Y C
S T G O E N S L C G T I D Q U
S N E H T A P W O U L D A S S
```

37. Fired

```
I T S P A C E C O U N T A K E
A G O A O N W O N K E D L O O
K A T M T O Y O L W H O L E I
F E E S I I I F C T T U A T I
O U N A N T S A I D G L E M E
T N O H I A U F M R N Y L I H
E I U U S G A R A E E T B S T
E T T L H I L M D C R D I T E
D N G T C L U I W H T T S A A
I O R T N B V Q V N S I N K E
E C O D A O S T N A O U O E G
O D W G R O W T H I L Q P N A
N D N P B T H P A E L U S E N
I K S I R L S P O U S E E E T
I T G O M C O N S I D E R E D
```

38. Forgiveness

```
S P I H S N O I T A L E R I A M
T S R U E T O M Y S D E L F T H
B Y E V I T A I T I N I F R E E
F O R N G I L A N O I T A R V A
I I M M E N S E N G M N T E S R
V N E R C V D Y O N S E T S A T
N S L A N O I T O M E D E I E N
V U S C A R S G U E R S N Y F E
T L H T V I R T R N S T T A G D
T Y I E H E E A O E T I I E R
M S T O I D S T E L F L O D E U
T A U N R T P H L H U E N R N B
I P A S G A E E T R A U M A S N
M D E V I E C R E P O F R W E U
E T B O L T T S I R V E I N N L
O V U N B U R Y G V I C T I M E
```

39. Potential

```
R I A D E R E T N E C S E L F
M E R E C R E A T I V E A E H
D L S G A L A C T I C I N N E
Z I A P E X A M P L E I M O A
I E V U O N G M W O L L A I L
S N U I T N Y F U E A F S S I
U E S N N H S S P I L E S S N
C R L S I E E I T P O A I E G
C G W T E V P N B R E R V R T
E Y C O N N E C T I O N E P C
S N T E L T I R E I L N I X E
S A E L O F A P S L C I G E L
N D D P I T N I P A A S T A F
E V I G R O F I M A L C A Y E
Z I B A L A N C E D H N S G R
```

40. Joy

```
K G C L U F Y O J I L T Y S T
E R N R L P I T N T U H L W O
Y R O I E I R N T H F I L O E
A O T W E A F A J N E N U R O
D U H Y E B T C O L T K F L O
Y T E H Y L F I B I A I E D C
R I R I O O S F V F R N O C
E N S O P S J I G E G G N H F
V E K W E S D N E I R F I A T
E S H R N T O G E I I L M L H
A M P R N O I I G D D I H I G
T X H E E U R S E R L E R V I
E I G H S C T N E Y N O W E R
F E E L S H T N G N I W O L F
```

41. Appreciation

```
I N T Y U M M Y S H I F T A M
A E T C S F I C D O O F A L S
F K L H E L O S O U L E P G M
F A A E O L L D W S I V P R O
I W T W O U F E P H A I R A S
R A R R A N G E M E N T E T S
M Y S P S R C H R S T C C I O
I T P M R I E E T R C A I T L
N U R I F A T I A F O N A U B
G A L I G N M E N T U F T D E
W E C E N I H S N U S L E E T
O B R L S E H S I R U O L F S
G N I V O L D E C I T O N Y A
I E U L A V E L T B U S F E T
```

42. Silent Counsel

```
I A N R S M P A U S E Y W W A
Y D A E R S H P L P G R I A E
T C I S T A E C T E I N T I L
G E M O Y S S N T T R E H T E
T L I L E F I A L A A T I C S
S N N U D X R L E L W G N Y N
E T E T Q T P R O P I E I T U
S N H I S D I E R M S T N I O
I E A O T U E G C E W I S L C
W L W N Q A T S R T M H I A B
N I K N F O P P I N I L R U E
G S I R E N N I U O I N A Q I
Y R E T S A M D A C P N G C N
E C A E P C E B R E A T H E G
```

43. Challenge

```
S I T A M L I S T E N I V I D
A M S W A K E N V I S I O N S
I X A L E R N G M Y W D H I R
E A P E M S D E D I U G A T N
D C B H R W O L L A U O O I S
I N R E G D E L W O N K C A Y
G B E H A V I O R S D R F T T
D O A M O N D H S R E E I I A
E T T L G A T E A A V L N O N
M R H N H K N W L O A E I N I
O U E S A I R I M U E A S Y F
N S E E S O Z S T T W S H H A
S T R U F E T C A C C E P T I
W B B A C H A L L E N G E N T
```

44. Setback

```
I M H E E T F O R G I V E T H
E T C A E R S C R I S K V H A
L L E N T S E E A G L R I E S
I N L I E R C F H R E T T E B
E W I C U O E M E B A T A D H
E Y C L V A O D A O R A G I E
S U I E M V W L D I N N E C D
S A R A I E A A O P I G N E E
F Y R N N L U O Y N E O D C
K D G S C I N T F G G R F O H
R Y T I L I B I S S O P O P O
P O N N R T R R E S P O N D O
U G N G I U T I I E X I S T S
T N A L P E S P O S I T I V E
T O G T O O L S E E D S R O W
```

45. Inherent Wisdom

```
H T U R T T S O U R C E I A L
U S O U N D N L A W I T H I N
M N I O O G W E M N Y I C N H
E L D N R R N E M I C O N T W
I E A E K I M I N O L H T S R
R Y D C R O G H S L M I O E U
O E M T D S E I E S U O F R N
I S T S A R T C N T E L G L I
U N I N E B T A N A E C E T V
I W N N E I I I N C L V C R E
D E T A V C M L T D E E N A R
S R A E T H I I L I E R E S
N W O L B E V O U T P N G H A
K N O W L E D G E O Y H G L L
I F E B O T T O M N E T S I L
```

46. Purpose

```
T N E L L E C X E Y D G I A E
L M T C S O C M L Y P N O L T
A E R I M E O I N O E P B A P
R N U G N R G A T S O M A A L
G O E N E S M N O A U K P H C
E I L I S I P P A H T P A O I
T T S Y C E R I W H R S N N M
A N I F T U R O R E C T O S P
T E M I P I R V C A R I U N O
I T P T G L T I I I T P H Y R
D N L N D E A L B C P I D P T
E I E E U T E U E O E O O R A
M P O D E E T R R S B E O N N
F M Y I F E I T L M L I F E T
E U L A V D I T E N A L P F E
```

47. Willingness

```
I Q A M W I L A U T I R I P S
T L U W L D E V R E S I E A P
H Y H I D N X G T O S X I R E
G T T L E M P P R N P O E T T
I I W L S T E E O A V E V I S
S N O I T A C I N U M M O C U
N U R N I G T D A E N D R I N
I M G G N N A S A V R E P P I
N M X P E I T N N I A G M A V
T O N T D G I O A E D M I T E
U C N Y K N O I T C E L F E R
I I P C G A N T U R E R R C S
T E E F P H S C R E A T E T E
U H U A L S K A E P I L E L S
C L A N G U A G E S K I L L S
```

48. Perception

```
F E E L I N G C I H C Y S P I
S A Y I N G R A E L C P S E A
S O V E R E I G N T Y R E T M
L R D P N I A V S I N O N I A
B G O E I O N M T P T T T H W
E H E R N T I H A L A E I W A
Y I G C R E G T H R P C W T R
O O F E M I T O I O D T E D E
N E L P L Y M H S U N E E R E
D A V T S E T I G R T D C V C
T O N I R T T I E I N N R Y A
R S C O L I N C S A E E I N F
U I N N V A S I P L S H O I R
T O U E S I P X O B A E R H U
H C E P D T E I O P O F N S S
```

49. Now

```
E F E E L Y T I N A Y T M R
F X U A A T T N M E O A I L
L Y P D W W S O E M V G T P
R E O E E A M E O S H E N S
H T S N R E R R L T E O S E
E E T C N I R E Y L I R M R
E Y A T H O E S N T U A P U
N T T R W E A N C E N F M T
E I S P T T C E C T S N I U
T R I A N H N K R I P S N F
E R E A T N H A E R N A D E
T H F H O S U C O F A G S N
C D N C Y E S T E R D A Y T
O W T R A F F I C Y E A R S
```

50. Trust

```
S E A L I N G I G S L E G N A
S G H C H T O N O O S S E T O
C R E T S M I I R W U N U S E
L O A U Y N A C T F O S T M M
A W R E R L A N F I E R B Y E
R T T A F P L I T I N R T X S
I H E L A E C A T R A I P H L
T Y O C N I R I C C A R F A Y
Y V I L E E R C I I E F U E S
E T N N L U E N O S D T K S D
Y N T E C B G S S U I A E O E
W I C E P N E I N R R C R G T
I C S A M E O I I U O A L O A
A N V E D N E P N R R I G H T
I S P A C E S D P G U I D E S
```

51. Going Within

```
I S A L G M N G E N E O I N G
W S I O A I T L W C E S H I N
T E I O A I T I I R N T O A I
S N Y T S B T T E O B M S L Y
G S S T U H O S I V A I B I C
S U E S I N R T E A T T I L
S O U N D L N O N L T U P S I
N I A G L E A W A R E N E S S
I C M H T L O E E Y R C C O H
N A I T C U I N R N Y N C U A
W P A E T B E T W E E N A R R
A S R W E V R E S E D R S C M
R E A R E F I L L N S E G E O
D R T H G I L S E N S E S Y N
D S S I L E N C E R E N N I Y
```

52. Trueness

```
I A T S T E N A L P G I A M O
S A N R D P E G A G N E E N A
S Y F G A N N D Y T I L A E R
E A T F E E E L U P D S C L O
N W L I E R H I R I N S R N E
E A I T C C T O R N E E E O L
U N T G S I T M Y F T R A I B
R N T T O E T A R E E P T T A
T O L N C W F N T S R X E A R
U Y E T O E E I E I P E V T E
S A I R E X H I N H O L O I N
F N G T P W L O E A T N L R L
G C F A M I L Y X P M U S R U
R E N R E V E A L E D E A I V
S D P A T H N O I S U L L I S
```

53. Choice

```
I C R H A P P I E R S F U L L
B A S E D S R D R H D D N I M
O O T R A T A E O C N S E V T
R O A D O C C N M O A Q T E A
K E R E K A T O E N S U T S H
F E T G I P I I P S U A A T T
H E O F N M C T V C O L I O
V C E A D I E I N I H I D B K
I N D N N G D E O T T S A C
H A P P E N I N G U S Y T H O
W T A R S G D O A S K L O F M
Y S S E S L O C F H G I H A N
D N O T H E S O O H C E R S A
L I L T H E T I D E V O L M E
```

54. Release

```
A W E S I Y E X P E C T R T E
L O Y F A T X E A G E N R D S
D L A A I I S R C D N O E P E
E F L T L L E I I I P I I A R
T S P T H I E U T P T R V P A
A G R E T B G I U U I C A I C
C N E N A I F S A T A R A L G
H I S T E S O L U E T T W R D
M S E I R N L A Y N N T I R P
E S N O B O L O O S E W A O A
N E T N W P R D J I R H E P N
T L M Y H S I G N O R I V E R
H B R E L E A S E N U E O E S
T G O F O R C E S S C O L D D
```

55. Expansion

```
S S U B T L E I M A M E X T P
A E W N D I N E N E R G Y E G
M I C I Y C D O E C I T O N L
N T J I T I S C S O I O A A I
U I S O T H N P A N E C S L G
S L A A U C I W S T C N D P H
R A T A R R A N G E M E N T T
E E X P I K N R L M V R A E H
S R T T E S I E P P N I L G O
M Y U N L O R V Y L E A L G U
N A I R E A L I Z A T I O N S
L N O I T A R G E T N I W I E
G B R I G H T L Y E D M E S N
E V O L Y L S H I F T E D N I
I N D A I L Y G N A T U R E H
H T F A C E T S M E T S Y S S
```

56. Faith

```
T N E I C N A P L A N E T T I
T E X E R C I S E S I R A R N
R U P S S U S T A I N S T U O
F L E S R U O Y H T I A F S I
B E R L M Y S T I C I S M T T
N O I T A D N U O F N I E V A
E N E A N S E I R E T S Y M T
C O N S C I O U S N E S S D I
O I C G N I M M A R G O R P M
N S E R H B U L W A R K A V I
J U N A E F P E R V A D E S L
U L I S A I T E V I T I S O P
R L V P N O I G I L E R H I N
E I I M P R O C E S S E H S A
Y S D N A P X E W O N K E L F
```

57. Happiness

```
I E B E A M T T O U C H H S A
P T A M P N D E P E N D E N T
Y A L O E C A L P R O C E S S
C T A T R A E H O O N M E E E
F S N I M I S E R A B L E X V
A O C O M F O R T A B L E P E
C U E N W H A S U S M I L E N
I T D A T M M G N I E B A R T
N S M L Y U N O I T A U T I S
G I Y I C C S A T I S F I E D
A D R R L A U T I R I P S N A
N E I G N I G N E L L A H C I
H C A A L A C I S Y H P N E L
D L D E I C E N T E R E D T Y
```

58. Gratitude

```
I A M I D N I W N O O M R N
S E G D E L W O N K C A G E
O H R T A E B A Y D D T C I
M T I U E R L R M I A I D N
S N E N E N R P A A T I O F
O I O A I A A N I C Z I L D
C G T C T N C N A C T I E Y
H H S S L E G R T A N E N R
T T P A L E P L S S P I T G
R M I N D H A N A H E A R T
A T R E X P E R I E N C E P
E N I A R S B E A T I N G I
D E T A V I T L U C Y D O B
S T N E S E R P S L O W L Y
```

59. Wholeness

```
U I A L M W W P F H P N O L
E N L I O A L E M L R A S C
D I A N O A A R O E E M T P
F I K R C R E N C H T L E H
W S V E T A G N P T E E P T
H E P I L I O T R A L L I A
O M O I N C C B A E P I E V
L N T G R E E U Y R M S C O
E Y W F I I L O L B O T A I
I T E N T L T D D A C E P C
H E N R A A L U L E T N S E
L E A M E D I T A T E E T H
R E S W O D A H S L A N D T
H M I N D I Y E N R U O J S
```

60. Connecting at the Heart Level

```
H R S M I L E F Y G R E N E
T E N I L N O I L T R E E S
A H A N I M A L S O A M C E
P G O N C L E A R N W E C D
T I I N G N I D N E S I G I
C H A F T P R E S E N T N U
T O A H E T I R I P S H E G
A C N T W O N D E R F U L T
E R T N T L S K C O R A R R
B R E C E I V I N G N A E U
N E L V E C T L W G E I T S
A H I O A L T U E H L L I T
M V I N V N Y L D N E I R F
U G T H G E S I N E T R I D
H N E P O S A R K A H C G S
```

188

Gratitude and Appreciation

This book reflects the creation of unity through diversity. Many people globally, spanning millennia, contributed to this project. Their talents and wisdom enhance the ineffable expression of the wordly wisdom of this Word Search Oracle.

Our brilliant Puzzle Master is Rick Smith. He carefully crafted each supremely soul satisfying puzzle. Loved that awesome book cover illustration and the sacred geometry nine pointed star puzzle logo? Also created by Rick. Additionally, he designed the book and made the whole brain illustration in *How to Play*.

All puzzle text Oracle messages are © Darity Wesley 2010-2017. They are used by permission. You may contact our Modern Day Oracle™ at www.DarityWesley.com

Vast waves of appreciation for her exquisitely extraordinary editorial contributions flow abundantly to Melissa Morgan. From the elimination of all extraneous words to creating the semi colon bump, she is a precious treasure in my writing process in addition to my life! You may contact her at www.HealingRocks.info or www.MMMHarp.com

We are deeply grateful to our significant others Bill Jurel and Erika Gilmore for giving us a loving foundation of nourishing support. We appreciate you!

Why the Eye?- Quote from Nikola Tesla from a talk called *On Light and Other High Frequency Phenomena* given at the Franklin Institute in 1893.

Introduction- View Of The North America From Space. Photo © Andrew7726

What is an Oracle?- Smoke On Black Background Photo © Vitalssss; Silhouette Of Man With Raised Hands Over Blur Cross Concept For Photo © Golfmhee

How to Use This Oracle- Mystery Photo © Americanmoustache

Let's Play!- Nerd Woman Photo © Vadimgozhda

How to Play- Opened Book With Rays Of Light Photo © Ksegev

The Yoga of Mantra- Glass Half Full ©Nexus7; Black And White Vector Henna Tatoo Mandala. OM Decorative Symbol Photo © Sunnylion

Why the Eye?- A Smiling Baby In Black And White Photo © Smartcoder; Futuristic Human Eye Photo © Dwnld777; The Eye Of Horus Photo © Eireanna; Iris Diagnosis Chart Eye Outline © Peter Hermes Furian

The Eyes of Horus- Isolated Figure Of Ancient Egypt God © Tansy; Yin Yang © Hospitalera; Moon Phases With Text Photo © Delstudio; All Seeing Eye Symbol Photo © Tomkovalcik; All-seeing eye, truncated pyramid closeup © Yauheni Hastsiukhin

Cristina's Commentary- Happiness © Stephen Coburn; Magic White Lotus Flower On Black Background Photo © Artnovielysa2

Your Brain on Word Search- Thinking Photo © Lassedesignen; Young Person Thinking With Glowing Puzzle

Mind © Ra2studio; Woman Reading Book Holding Torch Photo © Andreypopov; Inventor Of A Helmet For Brain Research © Andreyuu

You Did It!- Fun and education © Doreen Salcher

End Game- Holding The Light Photo © Petarpaunchev; Concept Greeting Card Of Opened Chest Treasure With Mystical Mir Photo © Alisali

Appreciation- Sphinx, beautiful ancient beast illustration © Ekaterina Gerasimova; Yin Yang on the beach © Kasparart

Gratitude- Human Hands Holding Jigsaw Puzzle Connection Concept Photo © Rawpixelimages

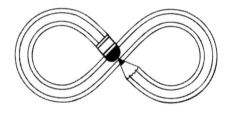

A big group hug of gratitude to our puzzle book play group- Bertha Edington, Denise Lewis Premschak, Ingrid Coffin, Jayne Sams, Lindsay Nakagawa, Patty Connor, Paula Wansley, and Wendy Kaveney.

Biographies

Darity Wesley

A "PuzzleGirl" since childhood, Darity Wesley loves playing with letters. Her fascination with all things word-wise, has helped her blossom throughout her life.

Spelling bees were drawn to Darity like a flower in school. No crossword puzzle, anagram, word search or any other word game was safe from her pencil and eraser. The years invested in gaining word wisdom through play served her well as a business lawyer. As a Modern Day Oracle™ and wisdom teacher, Darity's joyfully nurtured lifelong love of language gets to flourish and bloom in beautiful new ways. She enjoys online word games with chums around the world as well as the occasional Sudoku (penciled, not electronic). Darity and her husband Bob have been known to enjoy a rousing good game of Mexican Train with friends. Choo Choo!

Melissa Morgan -Editor Extraordinaire

Growing up, my grandfather, who we called Papa Judge, always had time for a game of dominos or several. We got to know and love each other through those drawn-out games. I went on to love Yahtzee and Boggle, spending many a hilarious evening with friends, dictionary in hand. It was always fascinating to see who ended up with which Boggle words!

I hadn't ever done a Sudoku until editing The Tao of Sudoku; now I am a convert! I find them to be surprisingly relaxing after a long day. My main puzzling love remains music; I am quite fond of the inside outwards forwards back approach to harmony. I've even been known to take a paintbrush to a music score to communicate the sense of what I hear.

Cristina and Rick Smith

Cristina and Rick spent their formative years playing games for hours upon hours together. Card games, jigsaw puzzles and board games were our favorites. Our parents encouraged us to be curious, creative and communicative. They gave us the tools, like lots of trips to the library, to nurture our intellects and discover answers for ourselves. They encouraged us to be independent thinkers. Most of all, they gave us the philosophical foundation that we could do anything we wanted.

At first glance, our shared underlying basis isn't easy to see as we are quite different personalities. We have embodied those principles in diverse seeming ways, yet we could be seen as two sides of a coin. In this book, Rick is the puzzle master and book designer. Cristina is the word smith and project orchestrator.

Rick has traveled the planet extensively and Cristina has traveled the inner worlds expansively. Rick developed some of the magic of today's technology and Cristina works the magic of subtle energy healing with people. Rick has worked with his community of longtime friends over the years to design and produce challengingly fun games and Cristina engages her community of longtime friends to create extraordinary events.

We have lots of fun when we get together, still doing puzzles and playing games. We are delighted you decided to play with us!

Also by Cristina and Rick Smith
The Tao of Sudoku- Yoga for the Brain
Invites You to Play!

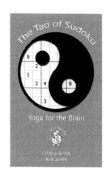

While I've never actually heard the term 'yoga for the brain' before, it makes total sense. This book easily fulfills the mental and spiritual aspects of a Yoga practice...So much more than a puzzle book, the fun facts, history, and education lining the pages make The Tao of Sudoku-Yoga for the Brain a unique treasure and I highly recommend it for an entertaining and enlightening experience! - *Reader Views*

Self-esteem in a Sudoku book! In airport bookshops, books of Sudoku number puzzles both taunted and repelled me in equal measure- not any more. With encouraging or enlightening sayings on each page, I was gently guided to let go of my old math phobic view of myself as puzzles began to unfold in a fun and challenging way. This book is fun and enlightening all at once, a real winner! - *Lauren McCall, author of The Eternal Gift*

The quotes on each page of The Tao of Sudoku-Yoga for the Brain are a personal coaching system designed to help readers beat discouragement, and think more deeply about their lives, ultimately helping them fine-tune their approach to finding their "path to enlightenment". As the authors quote Lao-Tzu with the first puzzle, "The journey of a thousand miles begins with a single step," and, in that spirit, this is a book worth starting and finishing. – *IndieReader*

Cristina and Rick Smith wrote a very witty and uplifting little book on how to use Sudoku as a spiritual practice. Very well done and entertaining. I really enjoyed it. Congratulations! - *Dr. Gaétan Chevalier, Director, The Earthing Institute*

This is a wonderful book with many life lessons under the Sudoku puzzles, along with quotes, fascinating facts and "how-to's" spread periodically throughout. <u>The Tao of Sudoku-Yoga for the Brain</u> is for anyone who enjoys puzzles and challenges for ages 14 and up. - *Chris Kyle (Age 16) for Reader Views Kids*

As a Yoga Teacher to those 50+, I'm all about Yoga for the Mind, Body and Spirit to keep us healthy and active as we age. I was intrigued by the concept of "Yoga for the Brain" using Sudoku and meditations. **What I found in <u>The Tao of Sudoku-Yoga for the Brain</u> is that it is much more than a numbers game. It is a journey into parts of ourselves yet to be explored. Give it a try!** - *Sherry Zak Morris, CEO Yoga Journey Productions*

I love Sudoku, especially the hard puzzles that challenge me. And I loved The Tao of Sudoku...Not because the puzzles themselves were particularly challenging but because this book challenged me in other ways. It challenged me to consider Sudoku not just as a fun hobby, but to use Sudoku as a meditative tool, too...**if you are looking for something that stretches your mind, nourishes your soul, and is entertaining and fun, this is the book for you. I recommend it unreservedly.** - *Readers' Favorite*

Winner of International Excellence Body, Mind, Spirit Book Award®
Winner of 2016-2017 Readers View Literary Award
Winner of 2016 New Apple Annual Book Award

49056543R00113

Made in the USA
San Bernardino, CA
11 May 2017